THE COWBOY'S PLAYBOOK

ON

CHINESE CHARACTER

TATTOOS

a tear-out reference for the West

80 high-frequency characters & phrases

two styles per entry · tear-out stencils · free companion site

(literally: tattoo dictionary)

刺青字典

The Cowboy's Playbook on Chinese Character Tattoos

compiled with pragmatism · printed for tearing

First edition, 2026

ISBN: 978-0-9891776-6-5

Foreword

This is a tear-out reference book. Each character occupies a
FOUR-PAGE block:
  - The EXPLANATION page on the front, with both Japanese-
    style and Chinese-style renderings (Yuji Boku and
    LXGW WenKai TC), full pronunciation (Mandarin pinyin
    plus Japanese on'yomi and kun'yomi), and a QR code
    to the companion site.
  - The THREE MORE STYLES page on the back of the
    explanation, showing the same character in three
    brushy variants for readers who want a calligraphic
    flourish.
  - The STENCIL or TRACE TEMPLATE page next, with three
    sizes side-by-side, MIRRORED for iron-on transfer.
  - A BLANK back so the stencil page can be torn, traced,
    or transferred without bleed-through.
We use traditional forms by default — the heart radical
心 inside 愛, the dragon's full body in 龍 — because that's
the version most readers find more charming.
This expanded edition covers sixty single characters and
twenty short phrases — eighty pieces of skin-ready Chinese
in total.

How to use this book

Each entry is FOUR pages.

PAGE 1 (recto) — explanation. Two style renderings
(Yuji Boku and LXGW WenKai TC).

PAGE 2 (verso) — three brushy variants for calligraphic
flair.

PAGE 3 (recto) — stencil. Three sizes mirrored for iron-on
transfer.

PAGE 4 (verso) — intentionally blank.

A note on style

Five font families per entry — two on the front, three on
the back.
JAPANESE STYLE (Yuji Boku 祐字墨) — heavy sumi-ink kaisho.
　　Used for the Japanese-style cell on the front page.
CHINESE STYLE (LXGW WenKai TC 霞鶩文楷) — traditional kaiti
　　regular script with full traditional coverage. The form
　　you'd take to the tattoo studio.
VERSO ROW 1 (Ma Shan Zheng 馬善政) — brushed semi-cursive,
　　simplified-Chinese only.
VERSO ROWS 2-3 (Liu Jian Mao Cao, Zhi Mang Xing) — running
　　script and wild cursive (also simp-only).
DISPLAY-LARGE characters (cover, title page, dividers) are
set in Source Han Serif TC for full traditional charm.

Cautionary tales

Verify with a native speaker, a CJK-experienced tattooist, AND a calligrapher if possible.

Search the character on this book's companion site to see it in alternate fonts and sizes before you ink.

If the character feels off in the mirror — listen to that.

Run it past someone who reads the language daily, not just Google Translate.

And remember: a great tattoo is one you've sat with for at least a few months. The book will still be here.

Companion website

Every entry in this book is also available online for free
at the address below. The site offers two extras the
printed page can't:

1. A FONT SELECTOR. Switch between Japanese-style (Yuji
   Boku), traditional kaiti (LXGW WenKai TC, the print
   default), brushed semi-cursive (Ma Shan Zheng),
   running script (Liu Jian Mao Cao), wild cursive (Zhi
   Mang Xing), and a Song-style serif fallback (Noto
   Serif CJK). See your character in the lineage you
   actually want before you ink.

2. DOWNLOADABLE STENCILS. Pick a size with a slider,
   choose mirrored or upright orientation, and download
   as PNG or PDF — sized to your body part of choice
   rather than the three preset sizes in this book.

Each entry in this book carries a QR code that links
straight to its page on the site.

https://kanji.xgar.com/

(intentionally blank — back of stencil page)

Part I · Single Characters

JAPANESE STYLE	CHINESE STYLE	PRONUNCIATION
(Yuji Boku)	(LXGW WenKai TC)	Mandarin

Mandarin

ài

On

アイ

Kun

いと(しい)・かな(しい)

MEANING

love

THE NUANCE

The traditional form of love. Carries the radical for heart right in the middle. The simplified form omits the heart - choose traditional for heart-on-sleeve sincerity.

SPOTTED ON

Worn by countless celebs and civilians alike. The most-tattooed Chinese character in the West. If in doubt, this is the safe pick.

HONORARY MENTION

Bai Ling has tattooed on her pubic mound she has spoken about it openly across magazine interviews. Holly Valance had inked down her bikini line in her early-2000s modeling years.

WHERE IT GOES

Wrist, inner forearm, ribcage, behind the ear.

WATCH OUT

Don't confuse with (shòu, to receive) - they look similar at small sizes.

THREE MORE STYLES

ài · love

BRUSH KAISHO

(Yuji Boku)

ROUNDED HANDWRITING

(Klee One)

TRAD SERIF

(Noto Serif TC)

(verso of explanation · stencil follows)

STENCIL OR TRACE TEMPLATE

ài · love

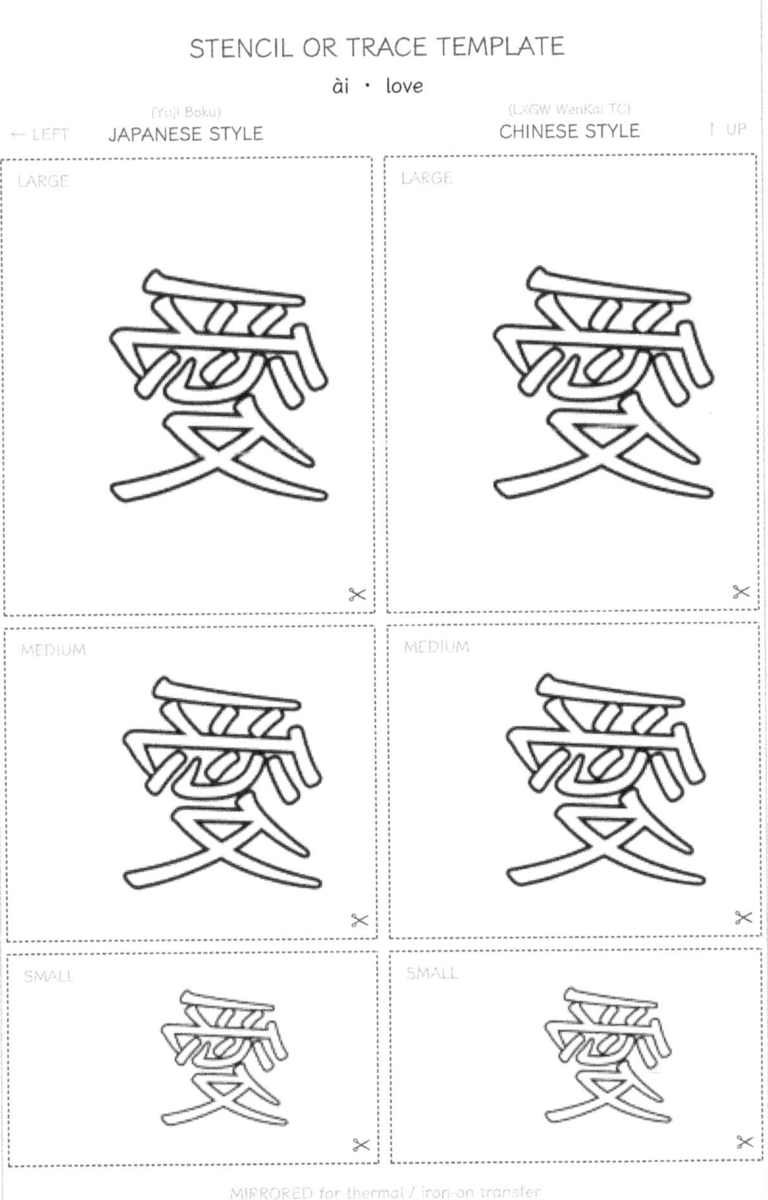

(intentionally blank — back of stencil page)

JAPANESE STYLE

(Yuji Boku)

CHINESE STYLE

(LXGW WenKai TC)

PRONUNCIATION

Mandarin

lóng

On

リュウ・リョウ

Kun

たつ

MEANING

dragon

THE NUANCE

Traditional form. Symbol of imperial power, strength, and good fortune. The Year of the Dragon is the most auspicious of the twelve.

SPOTTED ON

Bruce Lee built his entire brand around - the character appears across his estate's logo. A martial-arts staple.

HONORARY MENTION

Bruce Lee turned into a brand the character runs across his estate's logo and his training-jacket. The single most-quoted dragon tattoo in martial-arts history.

WHERE IT GOES

Back, full sleeve, chest plate. This character earns its real estate.

WATCH OUT

Simplified form is - much easier to ink, less ceremonial. Pick based on the energy you want.

THREE MORE STYLES

lóng · *dragon*

BRUSH KAISHO

(Yuji Boku)

ROUNDED HANDWRITING

(Klee One)

TRAD SERIF

(Noto Serif TC)

(verso of explanation · stencil follows)

STENCIL OR TRACE TEMPLATE

lóng · dragon

(Yuji Boku)
JAPANESE STYLE

(LXGW WenKai TC)
CHINESE STYLE

← LEFT

↑ UP

LARGE

LARGE

MEDIUM

MEDIUM

SMALL

SMALL

MIRRORED for thermal / iron-on transfer
snip along ✂ dotted lines · traditional Chinese throughout

(intentionally blank — back of stencil page)

JAPANESE STYLE	CHINESE STYLE	PRONUNCIATION
(Yuji Boku)	(LXGW WenKai TC)	Mandarin

Mandarin

hǔ

On
コ

Kun
とら

MEANING

tiger

THE NUANCE
Pure courage and authority. In Chinese culture, the tiger
is king of the beasts (the dragon rules the sky, the tiger
rules the earth).

SPOTTED ON
Common companion piece to a tattoo - dragon and tiger ( )
is a classic balance pairing in martial arts schools.

HONORARY MENTION
Mike Tyson sports a Bengal tiger across his right forearm
(per his Wikipedia tattoo entry). UFC's Dustin Poirier
wears bushido kanji running between the tiger stripes on
his left pec.

WHERE IT GOES
Shoulder blade, calf, outer forearm. Looks great on
muscular surfaces.

WATCH OUT
Don't pair with cute imagery - is fierce, not kitten
energy.

THREE MORE STYLES

hǔ · tiger

BRUSH KAISHO

(Yuji Boku)

ROUNDED HANDWRITING

(Klee One)

TRAD SERIF

(Noto Serif TC)

STENCIL OR TRACE TEMPLATE

hŭ · tiger

(Yuji Boku)
← LEFT   JAPANESE STYLE

(LXGW WenKai TC)
CHINESE STYLE   ↑ UP

LARGE

LARGE

MEDIUM

MEDIUM

SMALL

SMALL

MIRRORED for thermal / iron-on transfer
snip along ✂ dotted lines · traditional Chinese throughout

(intentionally blank — back of stencil page)

JAPANESE STYLE
(Yuji Boku)

CHINESE STYLE
(LXGW WenKai TC)

PRONUNCIATION

Mandarin

lì

On

リョク・リキ

Kun

ちから

MEANING

strength, power,

THE NUANCE
Two strokes. Maximum impact. The simplest way to put strength on your body in Chinese.

SPOTTED ON
Mel C of the Spice Girls famously wore (girl power) on her shoulder - the public face of 90s feminism in CJK form.

HONORARY MENTION
Mary J. Blige has (strength) on the back of her right hand got it before her No More Drama era. Mel C of the Spice Girls famously wore (girl power) on her shoulder during the 90s.

WHERE IT GOES
Bicep, deltoid, forearm. This one wants to be seen flexing.

WATCH OUT
Easy to mirror or rotate by mistake - confirm the orientation before the needle goes in.

THREE MORE STYLES

lì · strength, power,

BRUSH KAISHO

(Yuji Boku)

ROUNDED HANDWRITING

(Klee One)

TRAD SERIF

(Noto Serif TC)

(verso of explanation · stencil follows)

STENCIL OR TRACE TEMPLATE

lì · strength, power,

(Yuji Boku)
JAPANESE STYLE

(LXGW WenKai TC)
CHINESE STYLE

← LEFT   ↑ UP

LARGE

LARGE

MEDIUM

MEDIUM

SMALL

SMALL

MIRRORED for thermal / iron-on transfer
snip along ✂ dotted lines · traditional Chinese throughout

(intentionally blank — back of stencil page)

JAPANESE STYLE	CHINESE STYLE	PRONUNCIATION
(Yuji Boku)	(LXGW WenKai TC)	Mandarin

Mandarin

xīn

On

シン

Kun

こころ

MEANING

heart, mind,

THE NUANCE

Means both the physical heart and the seat of feeling and thinking. In classical Chinese, the heart IS the mind.

SPOTTED ON

A favorite minimalist tattoo. Often paired with a partner's name or worn solo on the wrist.

HONORARY MENTION

Ubiquitous on inner-wrists across the recovery, sobriety, and grief-tattoo crowd. No single celebrity bearer of the character solo is documented in mainstream press. Reader submissions welcome.

WHERE IT GOES

Inner wrist, sternum, back of neck. Tiny version sits well on a finger.

WATCH OUT

The four dots on the left side need clean spacing - a sloppy hand turns into a smudge.

THREE MORE STYLES

xīn · *heart, mind,*

BRUSH KAISHO

(Yuji Boku)

ROUNDED HANDWRITING

(Klee One)

TRAD SERIF

(Noto Serif TC)

(verso of explanation · stencil follows)

STENCIL OR TRACE TEMPLATE

xīn · heart, mind,

(Yuji Boku)
JAPANESE STYLE

(LXGW WenKai TC)
CHINESE STYLE

← LEFT ↑ UP

LARGE

LARGE

MEDIUM

MEDIUM

SMALL

SMALL

MIRRORED for thermal / iron-on transfer
snip along ✄ dotted lines · traditional Chinese throughout

JAPANESE STYLE	CHINESE STYLE	PRONUNCIATION
(Yuji Boku)	(LXGW WenKai TC)	Mandarin

fú

On

フク

Kun

さいわ(い)

MEANING

good fortune,

THE NUANCE
The character pasted upside-down on Chinese doorways at New Year (because upside down sounds like arrives). Pure positive vibes.

SPOTTED ON
Pink (the singer) had a character on her neck for years - close cousin of in the lucky-fortunate family.

HONORARY MENTION
Pink (the singer) has had a kanji (good fortune close cousin of) on her left foot since age 12. One of her oldest tattoos.

WHERE IT GOES
Anywhere visible - it's a charm, so let it work.

WATCH OUT
Some traditionalists tattoo it upside-down as a pun. Make sure your tattooist knows this is intentional, not a mistake.

THREE MORE STYLES

fú · *good fortune,*

BRUSH KAISHO

(Yuji Boku)

ROUNDED HANDWRITING

(Klee One)

TRAD SERIF

(Noto Serif TC)

(verso of explanation · stencil follows)

STENCIL OR TRACE TEMPLATE

fú · *good fortune,*

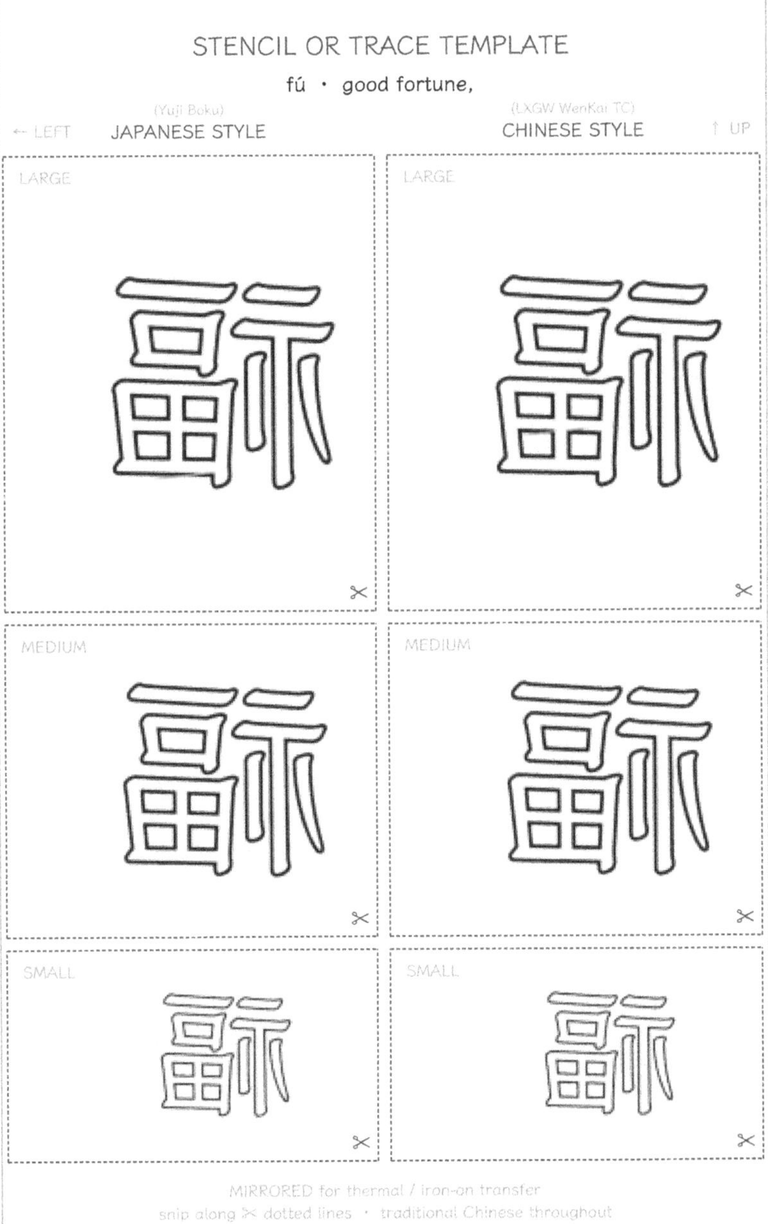

(intentionally blank — back of stencil page)

JAPANESE STYLE	CHINESE STYLE	PRONUNCIATION
(Yuji Boku)	(LXGW WenKai TC)	Mandarin

dào

On

ドウ・トウ

Kun

みち

MEANING

the way, path, the

THE NUANCE

The central concept of Taoism (and a borrowed cornerstone of Zen). Means literal road AND the deepest principle of how the universe works.

SPOTTED ON

Worn by martial artists, philosophers, and seekers across the West - from dojos in Texas to yoga studios in Brooklyn.

HONORARY MENTION

Standard issue across BJJ academies and judo dojos worldwide most students of the way wear it small at some point. No single celebrity bearer of solo is documented in major press.

WHERE IT GOES

Forearm, spine, shoulder. A walking character - it suits limbs.

WATCH OUT

Don't tattoo if you've never read a page of Lao Tzu. People will ask.

THREE MORE STYLES

dào · the way, path, the

BRUSH KAISHO

(Yuji Boku)

ROUNDED HANDWRITING

(Klee One)

TRAD SERIF

(Noto Serif TC)

(verso of explanation · stencil follows)

STENCIL OR TRACE TEMPLATE

dào · the way, path, the

(Yuji Boku)	(LXGW WenKai TC)
← LEFT JAPANESE STYLE	CHINESE STYLE ↑ UP

LARGE

LARGE

MEDIUM

MEDIUM

SMALL

SMALL

MIRRORED for thermal / iron-on transfer
snip along ✂ dotted lines · traditional Chinese throughout

← LEFT   JAPANESE STYLE   CHINESE STYLE   ↑ UP

(intentionally blank — back of stencil page)

JAPANESE STYLE	CHINESE STYLE	PRONUNCIATION
(Yuji Boku)	(LXGW WenKai TC)	Mandarin

PRONUNCIATION

Mandarin

rěn

On

ニン

Kun

しの(ぶ)・しの(ばせる)

MEANING

endure, patience,

THE NUANCE
Literally a knife over a heart - a blade on the heart is
the picture of endurance. The of ninja ( ).

SPOTTED ON
Standard issue at any martial arts gym. Worn by
mixed-martial-arts fighters as a vow to stay on the mat
when it hurts.

HONORARY MENTION
Ninja-Warrior-style tattoo across MMA gyms Renzo Gracie
and Eddie Bravo BJJ branches put it on banners and
hoodies. No single celebrity bearer of solo verified in
press.

WHERE IT GOES
Sternum, ribs, fist - somewhere it will literally hurt to
get tattooed. Fits the meaning.

WATCH OUT
Means patience more than tough guy. If you want pure
aggression, pick instead.

THREE MORE STYLES

rěn · endure, patience,

BRUSH KAISHO

(Yuji Boku)

ROUNDED HANDWRITING

(Klee One)

TRAD SERIF

(Noto Serif TC)

(verso of explanation · stencil follows)

STENCIL OR TRACE TEMPLATE

rěn · endure, patience,

(Yuji Boku)   (LXGW WenKai TC)

← LEFT   JAPANESE STYLE   CHINESE STYLE   ↑ UP

LARGE   LARGE

MEDIUM   MEDIUM

SMALL   SMALL

MIRRORED for thermal / iron-on transfer
snip along ✂ dotted lines · traditional Chinese throughout

JAPANESE STYLE	CHINESE STYLE	PRONUNCIATION
(Yuji Boku)	(LXGW WenKai TC)	Mandarin

wǔ

On

ブ・ム

Kun

たけ・たけ(し)

MEANING

martial, military,

THE NUANCE
The of kung fu ( ) and wushu ( ). The character is built from stop and spear - the warrior who STOPS the spear.

SPOTTED ON
Inked across MMA, BJJ, and karate communities. Joey Lawrence has (warrior) on his shoulder.

HONORARY MENTION
Joey Lawrence has (warrior) inked on his shoulder the lives in that compound. The character is also ubiquitous on UFC Open Workout backdrops at events in Asia.

WHERE IT GOES
Bicep, chest, back of forearm. Pairs well with (the warrior's way).

WATCH OUT
It's a serious character - not a costume. Earn it before you wear it.

THREE MORE STYLES

wǔ · martial, military,

BRUSH KAISHO

(Yuji Boku)

ROUNDED HANDWRITING

(Klee One)

TRAD SERIF

(Noto Serif TC)

(verso of explanation · stencil follows)

STENCIL OR TRACE TEMPLATE

wǔ · martial, military,

(Yuji Boku)
JAPANESE STYLE

(LXGW WenKai TC)
CHINESE STYLE

LARGE

LARGE

MEDIUM

MEDIUM

SMALL

SMALL

MIRRORED for thermal / iron-on transfer
snip along ✂ dotted lines · traditional Chinese throughout

JAPANESE STYLE	CHINESE STYLE	PRONUNCIATION
(Yuji Boku)	(LXGW WenKai TC)	Mandarin

yǒng

On

エイ

Kun

なが(い)

MEANING

eternal, forever

THE NUANCE

In Chinese calligraphy training, this single character contains all eight basic brushstrokes - so calligraphers literally practice life-long discipline through it.

SPOTTED ON

A common memorial tattoo. Often paired with a date or another character (= eternal love, = forever).

HONORARY MENTION

A common memorial tattoo, often paired with a date. No single celebrity bearer of solo is documented in mainstream press as of this printing.

WHERE IT GOES

Inner forearm, wrist, sternum. A forever character belongs somewhere you'll see daily.

WATCH OUT

Calligraphers will scrutinize this one - get a clean source, not a Microsoft Word printout.

THREE MORE STYLES

yǒng · eternal, forever

BRUSH KAISHO

(Yuji Boku)

ROUNDED HANDWRITING

(Klee One)

TRAD SERIF

(Noto Serif TC)

(verso of explanation · stencil follows)

STENCIL OR TRACE TEMPLATE

yǒng · eternal, forever

(Yuji Boku)	(LXGW WenKai TC)
← LEFT JAPANESE STYLE	CHINESE STYLE ↑ UP

LARGE

LARGE

MEDIUM

MEDIUM

SMALL

SMALL

MIRRORED for thermal / iron-on transfer
snip along ✂ dotted lines · traditional Chinese throughout

(intentionally blank — back of stencil page)

JAPANESE STYLE	CHINESE STYLE	PRONUNCIATION
(Yuji Boku)	(LXGW WenKai TC)	Mandarin

mèng

On

ム・ボウ

Kun

ゆめ

MEANING

dream, vision

THE NUANCE

The character sits under the radical for evening - dreams
happen at night. Both literal sleep-dreams and
life-aspirations.

SPOTTED ON

Common pick for artists, musicians, and entrepreneurs.
Trace its appeal back to follow your dreams generation.

HONORARY MENTION

Demetrious 'Mighty Mouse' Johnson UFC and ONE Championship
flyweight champion has inked across the center of his
chest.

WHERE IT GOES

Shoulder, thigh, behind the ear. A character that wants
soft skin.

WATCH OUT

Simplified is - much cleaner. Traditional has more strokes
but more romance.

THREE MORE STYLES

mèng · dream, vision

BRUSH KAISHO

(Yuji Boku)

ROUNDED HANDWRITING

(Klee One)

TRAD SERIF

(Noto Serif TC)

(verso of explanation · stencil follows)

STENCIL OR TRACE TEMPLATE

mèng · dream, vision

(Yuji Boku)
(LXGW WenKai TC)

← LEFT   **JAPANESE STYLE**   **CHINESE STYLE**   ↑ UP

LARGE   LARGE

MEDIUM   MEDIUM

LARGE   LARGE

SMALL   SMALL

MIRRORED for thermal / iron-on transfer
snip along ✂ dotted lines · traditional Chinese throughout

(intentionally blank — back of stencil page)

JAPANESE STYLE	CHINESE STYLE	PRONUNCIATION
(Yuji Boku)	(LXGW WenKai TC)	Mandarin

yǒng

On
ユウ

Kun
いさ(む)・いさ(ましい)

MEANING

courage, bravery

THE NUANCE
Different y ng from (eternal) - same sound, different character. This one means guts.

SPOTTED ON
Worn by veterans, first responders, and anyone who has pulled themselves out of a hard year.

HONORARY MENTION
Angelina Jolie and her then-husband Jonny Lee Miller got matching tattoos during their 1996 marriage. She had hers removed years later.

WHERE IT GOES
Chest, bicep, calf. A combat-position character.

WATCH OUT
The (strength) at the bottom needs clean strokes - don't let your tattooist rush it.

THREE MORE STYLES

yǒng · courage, bravery

BRUSH KAISHO

(Yuji Boku)

ROUNDED HANDWRITING

(Klee One)

TRAD SERIF

(Noto Serif TC)

STENCIL OR TRACE TEMPLATE

yǒng · courage, bravery

<table>
<tr><td>← LEFT   (Yuji Boku)
JAPANESE STYLE</td><td>(LXGW WenKai TC)
CHINESE STYLE   ↑ UP</td></tr>
</table>

JAPANESE STYLE	CHINESE STYLE
LARGE	LARGE
MEDIUM	MEDIUM
SMALL	SMALL

MIRRORED for thermal / iron-on transfer
snip along ✂ dotted lines · traditional Chinese throughout

(intentionally blank — back of stencil page)

JAPANESE STYLE	CHINESE STYLE	PRONUNCIATION
(Yuji Boku)	(LXGW WenKai TC)	Mandarin

chán

On
ゼン

Kun
—

MEANING

Zen, meditation

THE NUANCE

The Chinese root of Japanese Zen (in simplified Japanese
form). The character of stillness - despite its 17
strokes.

SPOTTED ON

Steve Jobs aesthetic religion in one character. Worn
across the wellness, design, and tech worlds.

HONORARY MENTION

Worn quietly across the wellness, design, and tech-founder
crowd (Steve-Jobs-aesthetic energy). No specific celebrity
bearer of the character solo verified.

WHERE IT GOES

Back of neck, between shoulder blades, inner forearm.
Quiet placements for a quiet character.

WATCH OUT

Make sure your tattooist gets the (single) component right
- it's the heart of the character.

THREE MORE STYLES

chán · Zen, meditation

BRUSH KAISHO

(Yuji Boku)

ROUNDED HANDWRITING

(Klee One)

TRAD SERIF

(Noto Serif TC)

(verso of explanation · stencil follows)

STENCIL OR TRACE TEMPLATE

chán · Zen, meditation

(Yuji Boku)	(LXGW WenKai TC)
← LEFT JAPANESE STYLE	CHINESE STYLE ↑ UP

LARGE

LARGE

MEDIUM

MEDIUM

SMALL

SMALL

(intentionally blank — back of stencil page)

JAPANESE STYLE	CHINESE STYLE	PRONUNCIATION
(Yuji Boku)	(LXGW WenKai TC)	Mandarin

yì

On

ギ

Kun

—

MEANING

honor,

THE NUANCE

The traditional form. Built from sheep over I/me sacrificing self to do what's right. Cornerstone Confucian virtue.

SPOTTED ON

Loyalty and honor characters have been a Lakers locker-room favorite for decades. Allen Iverson famously had (loyalty) on his neck - same family.

HONORARY MENTION

Allen Iverson has the close-cousin (loyalty) on the right side of his neck same Confucian-virtue family. Together with , the pair forms the wuxia-hero motto.

WHERE IT GOES

Shoulder, back, ribs. A heavy character that wants a bold canvas.

WATCH OUT

Simplified is much smaller (3 strokes) - lacks the gravitas. Go traditional or go home.

THREE MORE STYLES

yì · honor,

BRUSH KAISHO

(Yuji Boku)

ROUNDED HANDWRITING

(Klee One)

TRAD SERIF

(Noto Serif TC)

STENCIL OR TRACE TEMPLATE

yì · honor,

<table>
<tr><td>(Yuji Boku)
← LEFT   JAPANESE STYLE</td><td>(LXGW WenKai TC)
CHINESE STYLE   ↑ UP</td></tr>
</table>

LARGE

LARGE

MEDIUM

MEDIUM

SMALL

SMALL

(intentionally blank — back of stencil page)

JAPANESE STYLE	CHINESE STYLE	PRONUNCIATION
(Yuji Boku)	(LXGW WenKai TC)	Mandarin

měi

On
ビ・ミ

Kun
うつく(しい)

MEANING

beauty, beautiful

THE NUANCE

Built from sheep over big - in ancient agrarian China, a big plump sheep was the picture of beauty. Goes back five thousand years.

SPOTTED ON

Common solo wrist tattoo. Also the in (America) - so doubles as a patriotic flex if you lean that way.

HONORARY MENTION

A K-pop and J-pop fan crowd wrist-tattoo classic common but anonymously borne. No single celebrity bearer documented in mainstream press.

WHERE IT GOES

Inner wrist, behind the ear, ankle. A character for delicate skin.

WATCH OUT

Don't combine with random characters thinking you're spelling beautiful person or similar - Chinese doesn't compose like English.

THREE MORE STYLES

měi · beauty, beautiful

BRUSH KAISHO

(Yuji Boku)

ROUNDED HANDWRITING

(Klee One)

TRAD SERIF

(Noto Serif TC)

STENCIL OR TRACE TEMPLATE

měi · beauty, beautiful

(Yuji Boku)

← LEFT   **JAPANESE STYLE**

(LXGW WenKai TC)

CHINESE STYLE   ↑ UP

LARGE

LARGE

MEDIUM

MEDIUM

SMALL

SMALL

MIRRORED for thermal / iron-on transfer
snip along ✂ dotted lines · traditional Chinese throughout

(intentionally blank — back of stencil page)

JAPANESE STYLE	CHINESE STYLE	PRONUNCIATION
(Yuji Boku)	(LXGW WenKai TC)	Mandarin

fēng

On

フウ・フ

Kun

かぜ・かざ

MEANING

wind

THE NUANCE
Traditional form. The of fong shui ( ). Movement,
freshness, the unseen force that shapes everything it
touches.

SPOTTED ON
Worn by surfers, sailors, and anyone who lives outdoors.
Common pairing with for a mini feng-shui statement.

HONORARY MENTION
A favorite of pro surfers, sailors, and the storm-chaser
tattoo crowd. No specific named celebrity bearer of solo
verified.

WHERE IT GOES
Calf, outer forearm, behind the shoulder. Fits well on a
moving body part.

WATCH OUT
Simplified is - very different look. Traditional carries
the insect radical inside, simplified is hollow.

THREE MORE STYLES

fēng · wind

BRUSH KAISHO

(Yuji Boku)

ROUNDED HANDWRITING

(Klee One)

TRAD SERIF

(Noto Serif TC)

(verso of explanation · stencil follows)

STENCIL OR TRACE TEMPLATE

fēng · wind

(Yuji Boku)	(LXGW WenKai TC)
← LEFT　JAPANESE STYLE	CHINESE STYLE　↑ UP

LARGE

LARGE

MEDIUM

MEDIUM

SMALL

SMALL

MIRRORED for thermal / iron-on transfer
snip along ✂ dotted lines · traditional Chinese throughout

(intentionally blank — back of stencil page)

JAPANESE STYLE	CHINESE STYLE	PRONUNCIATION
(Yuji Boku)	(LXGW WenKai TC)	Mandarin

Mandarin

huǒ

On

カ

Kun

ひ・ほ

MEANING

fire

THE NUANCE
Four strokes. One of the five elements ( ). Looks like a
stick figure with arms raised - the original pictograph.

SPOTTED ON
Common solo piece in the metal/punk crowd. Also seen as
over a ribcage piece for fire-in-the-belly types.

HONORARY MENTION
Found across the metal/punk scene and ribcage tattoo
culture. No specific named celebrity bearer of solo
verified.

WHERE IT GOES
Chest, ribs, ankle. A character with kinetic energy -
place it where it can move.

WATCH OUT
Pairs aggressively with (dragon) - reads as fire dragon.
Make sure that's the energy you want.

THREE MORE STYLES

huǒ · fire

BRUSH KAISHO

(Yuji Boku)

ROUNDED HANDWRITING

(Klee One)

TRAD SERIF

(Noto Serif TC)

(verso of explanation · stencil follows)

STENCIL OR TRACE TEMPLATE

huǒ · fire

(Yuji Boku)
(LXGW WenKai TC)

← LEFT **JAPANESE STYLE** **CHINESE STYLE** ↑ UP

LARGE

LARGE

MEDIUM

MEDIUM

SMALL

SMALL

MIRRORED for thermal / iron-on transfer
snip along ✂ dotted lines · traditional Chinese throughout

(intentionally blank — back of stencil page)

JAPANESE STYLE	CHINESE STYLE	PRONUNCIATION
(Yuji Boku)	(LXGW WenKai TC)	Mandarin

shuǐ

On
スイ

Kun
みず

MEANING

water

THE NUANCE
Another of the five elements. Bruce Lee's be water philosophy made this a Western tattoo classic. Adaptable, formless, unstoppable.

SPOTTED ON
Surfers, swimmers, BJJ players (water in jiu-jitsu is a teaching metaphor). Often paired with or .

HONORARY MENTION
Inked across the BJJ community as a Bruce Lee 'be water' nod. Common in Eddie Bravo's 10th Planet system. No single named bearer verified.

WHERE IT GOES
Wrist, ankle, ribs. A flowing character - place it where the body bends.

WATCH OUT
Looks deceptively simple - but the four strokes need balance. A rushed looks like a smudge.

THREE MORE STYLES

shuǐ · water

BRUSH KAISHO

(Yuji Boku)

ROUNDED HANDWRITING

(Klee One)

TRAD SERIF

(Noto Serif TC)

(verso of explanation · stencil follows)

STENCIL OR TRACE TEMPLATE
shuǐ · water

(Yuji Boku)
JAPANESE STYLE

(LXGW WenKai TC)
CHINESE STYLE

LARGE

LARGE

MEDIUM

MEDIUM

SMALL

SMALL

MIRRORED for thermal / iron-on transfer
snip along ✂ dotted lines · traditional Chinese throughout

JAPANESE STYLE	CHINESE STYLE	PRONUNCIATION
(Yuji Boku)	(LXGW WenKai TC)	Mandarin

yuè

On

ゲツ・ガツ

Kun

つき

MEANING

moon, month

THE NUANCE

Pictograph of a crescent moon. Doubles as the word for month - because the lunar cycle measures the month in Chinese.

SPOTTED ON

A favorite of the celestial-tattoo crowd. Often paired with (sun) on opposite wrists or shoulders.

HONORARY MENTION

Common pair-tattoo with (sun) on opposite wrists or shoulders. No specific celebrity bearer of solo verified.

WHERE IT GOES

Inner wrist, behind the ear, ankle. A delicate-skin character.

WATCH OUT

Easy to confuse with (sun) at small sizes - the has two horizontal strokes inside, has one.

THREE MORE STYLES

yuè · moon, month

BRUSH KAISHO

(Yuji Boku)

ROUNDED HANDWRITING

(Klee One)

TRAD SERIF

(Noto Serif TC)

(verso of explanation · stencil follows)

STENCIL OR TRACE TEMPLATE

yuè · moon, month

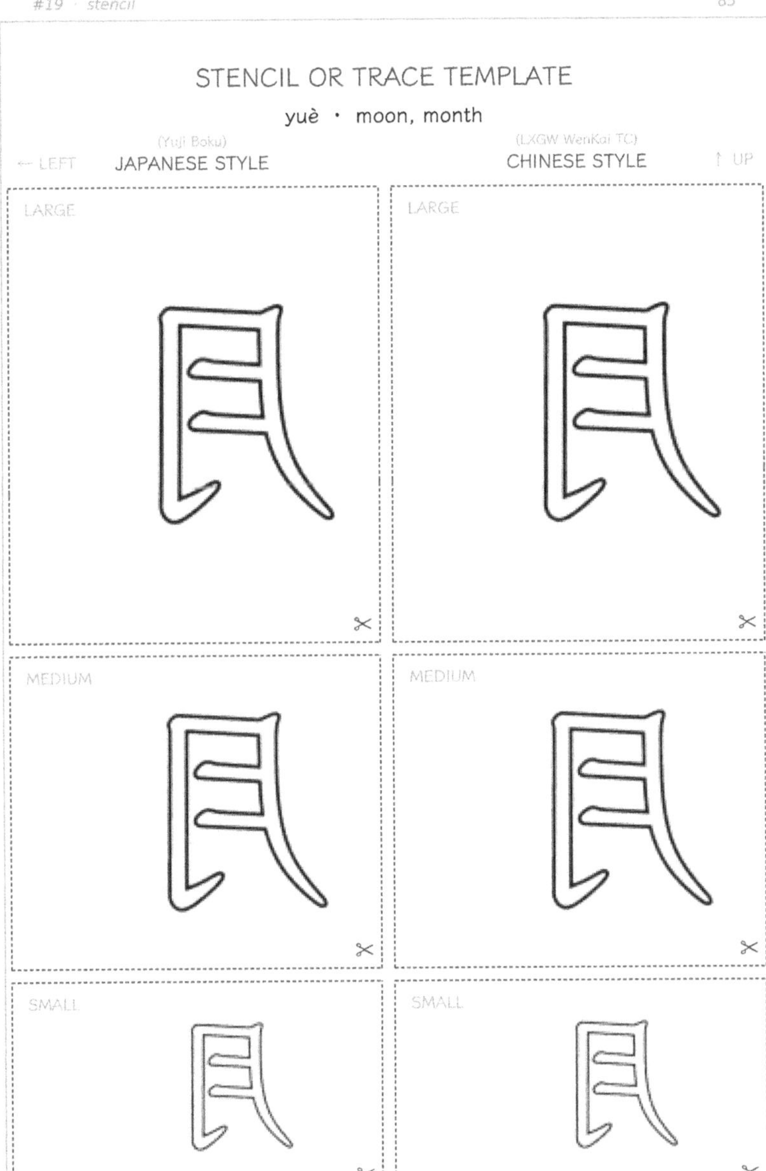

(intentionally blank — back of stencil page)

JAPANESE STYLE	CHINESE STYLE	PRONUNCIATION
(Yuji Boku)	(LXGW WenKai TC)	Mandarin

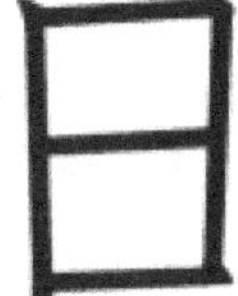

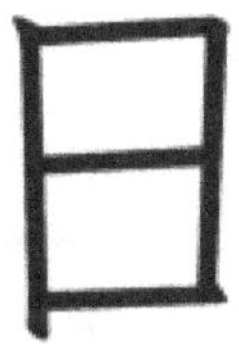

rì

On

ニチ・ジツ

Kun

ひ・か

MEANING

sun, day

THE NUANCE
Pictograph of the sun (originally drawn as a circle with a dot inside). Also means day, as in measure of time.

SPOTTED ON
Often inked on the body opposite a - day and night, light and shadow. The in (Japan).

HONORARY MENTION
See the day/night pair tattoo is widespread but anonymously borne. No specific celebrity bearer of solo verified.

WHERE IT GOES
Wrist, ankle, behind the ear. Pairs visually with the moon.

WATCH OUT
Three strokes only - so symmetry matters. A wonky looks like a wonky window frame.

THREE MORE STYLES

rì · sun, day

BRUSH KAISHO

(Yuji Boku)

ROUNDED HANDWRITING

(Klee One)

TRAD SERIF

(Noto Serif TC)

STENCIL OR TRACE TEMPLATE

rì · sun, day

(Yuji Boku)
JAPANESE STYLE

(LXGW WenKai TC)
CHINESE STYLE

← LEFT

↑ UP

LARGE

LARGE

MEDIUM

MEDIUM

SMALL

SMALL

JAPANESE STYLE	CHINESE STYLE	PRONUNCIATION
(Yuji Boku)	(LXGW WenKai TC)	Mandarin

xīng

On

セイ・ショウ

Kun

ほし

MEANING

star

THE NUANCE
Built from sun on top and birth below - the thing born of light. A small character that punches above its weight.

SPOTTED ON
Common solo wrist tattoo. Also worn as a constellation reference - (North Star) for sailors and seekers.

HONORARY MENTION
A small wrist-tattoo classic; often part of a star-cluster constellation piece. No specific celebrity bearer of solo documented.

WHERE IT GOES
Inner wrist, behind the ear, sternum. A small-canvas character.

WATCH OUT
Looks similar to (to be) at glance - confirm strokes with your tattooist before the needle drops.

THREE MORE STYLES

xīng · star

BRUSH KAISHO

(Yuji Boku)

ROUNDED HANDWRITING

(Klee One)

TRAD SERIF

(Noto Serif TC)

(verso of explanation · stencil follows)

STENCIL OR TRACE TEMPLATE

xīng · star

(Yuji Boku)
(LXGW WenKai TC)

← LEFT **JAPANESE STYLE**   **CHINESE STYLE**   ↑ UP

LARGE

LARGE

MEDIUM

MEDIUM

SMALL

SMALL

MIRRORED for thermal / iron-on transfer
snip along ✂ dotted lines · traditional Chinese throughout

(intentionally blank — back of stencil page)

JAPANESE STYLE	CHINESE STYLE	PRONUNCIATION
(Yuji Boku)	(LXGW WenKai TC)	Mandarin

shān

On
サン

Kun
やま

MEANING

mountain

THE NUANCE
Three peaks. The simplest pictograph in the language and the most universally legible. Steady, immovable, ancient.

SPOTTED ON
Climbers, hikers, and the mountain-as-life-metaphor crowd. A staple in the outdoor community.

HONORARY MENTION
Worn widely across the climbing and hiking community three peaks, one pictograph. No specific celebrity bearer documented.

WHERE IT GOES
Wrist, sternum, between shoulder blades. Looks great large OR small.

WATCH OUT
Three vertical strokes need EVEN spacing - uneven reads as broken teeth, not mountain.

THREE MORE STYLES

shān · mountain

BRUSH KAISHO

(Yuji Boku)

ROUNDED HANDWRITING

(Klee One)

TRAD SERIF

(Noto Serif TC)

(verso of explanation · stencil follows)

STENCIL OR TRACE TEMPLATE

shān · mountain

(Yuji Boku)   (LXGW WenKai TC)
← LEFT   **JAPANESE STYLE**   **CHINESE STYLE**   ↑ UP

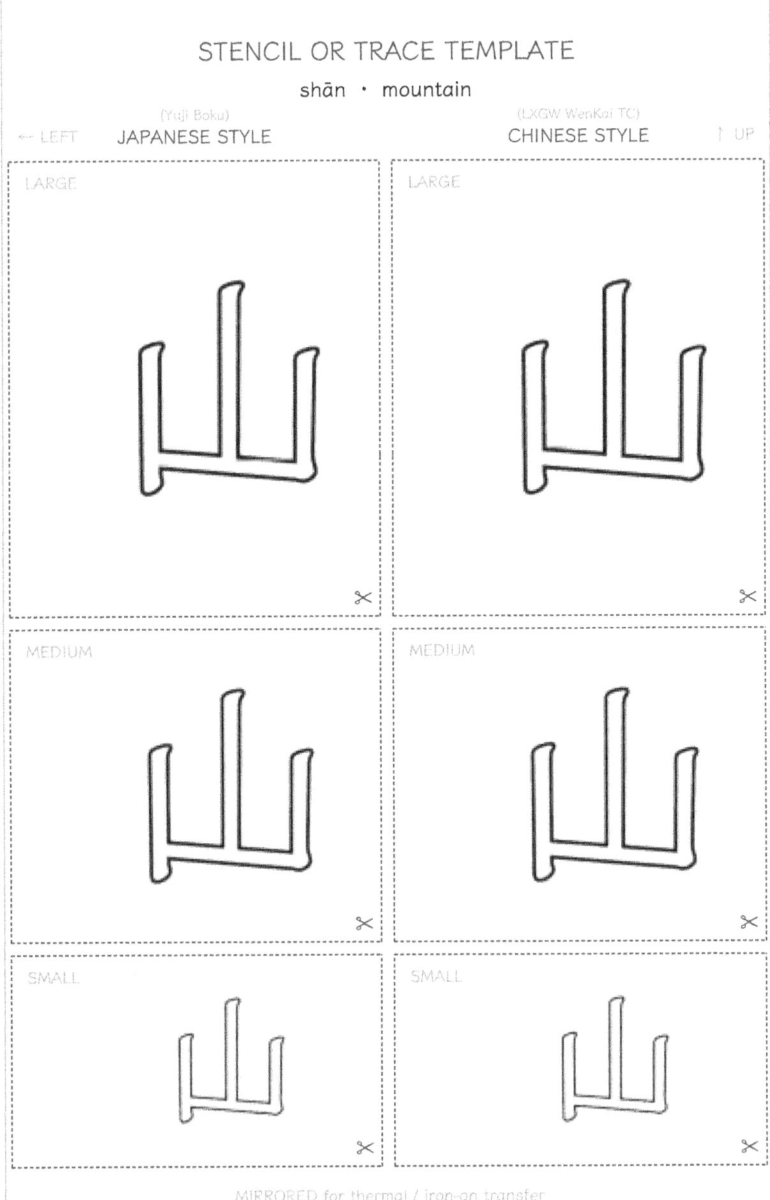

MIRRORED for thermal / iron-on transfer
snip along ✂ dotted lines · traditional Chinese throughout

(intentionally blank — back of stencil page)

JAPANESE STYLE	CHINESE STYLE	PRONUNCIATION
(Yuji Boku)	(LXGW WenKai TC)	Mandarin

hǎi

On
カイ

Kun
うみ

MEANING

sea, ocean

THE NUANCE

Water radical plus (every) - every body of water flows here. The Pacific and Atlantic both end up in .

SPOTTED ON

Worn by sailors, surfers, divers, and the ocean-cleanup crowd. Sometimes paired with - mountain and sea.

HONORARY MENTION

Common among Pacific surfers, divers, and the ocean-cleanup crowd. No specific celebrity bearer of solo documented.

WHERE IT GOES

Bicep, ribcage, calf. A character that wants room to breathe.

WATCH OUT

Don't pair with random water-themed Chinese - is general ocean, not your specific lake or river.

THREE MORE STYLES

hǎi · *sea, ocean*

BRUSH KAISHO

(Yuji Boku)

ROUNDED HANDWRITING

(Klee One)

TRAD SERIF

(Noto Serif TC)

(verso of explanation · stencil follows)

STENCIL OR TRACE TEMPLATE

hǎi · sea, ocean

(Yuji Boku)   (LXGW WenKai TC)

← LEFT   **JAPANESE STYLE**   **CHINESE STYLE**   ↑ UP

LARGE   LARGE

MEDIUM   MEDIUM

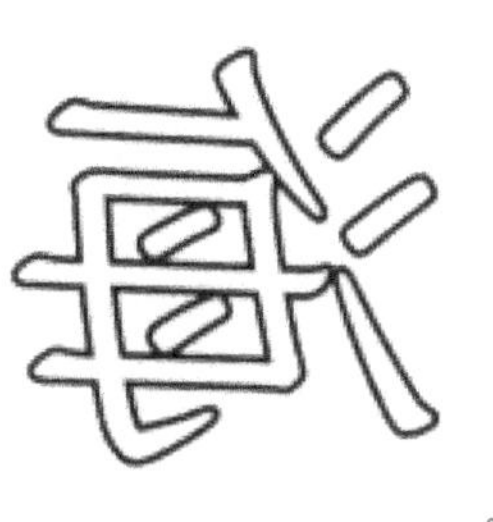

SMALL   SMALL

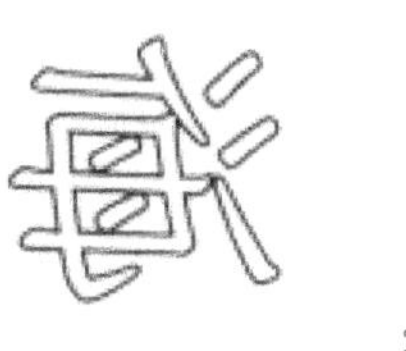

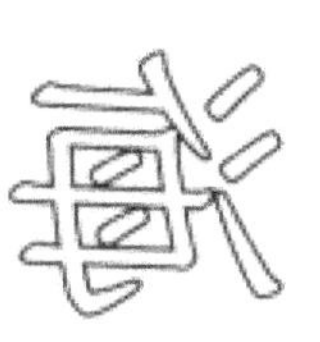

MIRRORED for thermal / iron-on transfer
snip along ✂ dotted lines · traditional Chinese throughout

(intentionally blank — back of stencil page)

JAPANESE STYLE
(Yuji Boku)

CHINESE STYLE
(LXGW WenKai TC)

PRONUNCIATION

Mandarin

tiān

On

テン

Kun

あめ・あま

MEANING

heaven, sky, day

THE NUANCE
Built from one (heaven's ceiling) over big (a person with arms outstretched) - the great expanse above. Means sky and heaven both.

SPOTTED ON
A favorite in spiritual and astronomy crowds. Also carries political weight - (mandate of heaven).

HONORARY MENTION
David Beckham has the Confucian Analects line (life-and-death are fated, fortune lies with heaven) running down his left flank ending in . Inked in 2008.

WHERE IT GOES
Sternum, between shoulder blades, inner forearm. A character that points up.

WATCH OUT
At small sizes can be confused with (husband) - they share the same skeleton. Confirm with your tattooist.

THREE MORE STYLES

tiān · heaven, sky, day

BRUSH KAISHO

(Yuji Boku)

ROUNDED HANDWRITING

(Klee One)

TRAD SERIF

(Noto Serif TC)

(verso of explanation · stencil follows)

STENCIL OR TRACE TEMPLATE

tiān · *heaven, sky, day*

(Yuji Boku)
(LXGW WenKai TC)

← LEFT   JAPANESE STYLE   CHINESE STYLE   ↑ UP

LARGE

LARGE

MEDIUM

MEDIUM

SMALL

SMALL

MIRRORED for thermal / iron-on transfer
snip along ✂ dotted lines · traditional Chinese throughout

JAPANESE STYLE

(Yuji Boku)

CHINESE STYLE

(LXGW WenKai TC)

PRONUNCIATION

Mandarin

shén

On

シン・ジン

Kun

かみ・かん

MEANING

god, spirit, divine

THE NUANCE

Worship radical plus (to state) - the divine that speaks.
Also the of (mind/spirit) - so doubles as inner spirit.

SPOTTED ON

Worn across martial arts, religious, and gaming
subcultures. The of Hayao Miyazaki's Spirited Away ( ).

HONORARY MENTION

Common across MMA, gaming, and wellness tattoo culture. No
specific named celebrity bearer of solo verified.

WHERE IT GOES

Sternum, between shoulder blades, inner bicep. Wants a
contemplative placement.

WATCH OUT

Tone is genuinely sacred - not a casual character. Be
ready for serious questions.

THREE MORE STYLES

shén · god, spirit, divine

BRUSH KAISHO

(Yuji Boku)

ROUNDED HANDWRITING

(Klee One)

TRAD SERIF

(Noto Serif TC)

(verso of explanation · stencil follows)

STENCIL OR TRACE TEMPLATE

shén · *god, spirit, divine*

(Yuji Boku)
JAPANESE STYLE

(LXGW WenKai TC)
CHINESE STYLE

← LEFT

↑ UP

LARGE

LARGE

MEDIUM

MEDIUM

LARGE

LARGE

SMALL

SMALL

(intentionally blank — back of stencil page)

JAPANESE STYLE	CHINESE STYLE	PRONUNCIATION
(Yuji Boku)	(LXGW WenKai TC)	Mandarin

fèng

On
ホウ

Kun
おおとり

MEANING

phoenix

THE NUANCE
The mythical phoenix - female counterpart to (dragon).
Together means perfect harmony, often inked by couples.

SPOTTED ON
A traditional bridal tattoo in some regions. Also seen
across the K-pop and J-pop fan crowd.

HONORARY MENTION
A traditional bridal pairing with couples in Hong Kong and
Taipei still ink the pair on wedding-day. No specific
celebrity bearer documented.

WHERE IT GOES
Back, shoulder blade, ribs. A character that earns canvas.

WATCH OUT
Simplified is - much smaller, much cleaner. Traditional
has 14 strokes and demands a steady hand.

THREE MORE STYLES

fèng · phoenix

BRUSH KAISHO

(Yuji Boku)

ROUNDED HANDWRITING

(Klee One)

TRAD SERIF

(Noto Serif TC)

(verso of explanation · stencil follows)

STENCIL OR TRACE TEMPLATE
fèng · phoenix

(Yuji Boku)	(LXGW WenKai TC)
← LEFT JAPANESE STYLE	CHINESE STYLE ↑ UP

LARGE

LARGE

MEDIUM

MEDIUM

SMALL

SMALL

MIRRORED for thermal / iron-on transfer
snip along ✂ dotted lines · traditional Chinese throughout

(intentionally blank — back of stencil page)

JAPANESE STYLE	CHINESE STYLE	PRONUNCIATION
(Yuji Boku)	(LXGW WenKai TC)	Mandarin

láng

On
ロウ

Kun
おおかみ

MEANING

wolf

THE NUANCE
Dog radical plus (good) - the noble dog. Symbol of ferocity, loyalty, and pack mentality.

SPOTTED ON
Common in motorcycle clubs, military units, and the lone-wolf-archetype crowd. Pairs with or .

HONORARY MENTION
Common in motorcycle clubs, military units, and the lone-wolf-archetype crowd. No specific named celebrity bearer documented in mainstream press.

WHERE IT GOES
Outer forearm, calf, shoulder blade. Looks great on muscular real estate.

WATCH OUT
Don't tattoo if you actually want man's best friend - that's (qu n) or (g u).

THREE MORE STYLES

láng · wolf

BRUSH KAISHO

(Yuji Boku)

ROUNDED HANDWRITING

(Kiee One)

TRAD SERIF

(Noto Serif TC)

(verso of explanation · stencil follows)

STENCIL OR TRACE TEMPLATE

láng · wolf

(Yuji Boku)
(LXGW WenKai TC)

← LEFT   **JAPANESE STYLE**   **CHINESE STYLE**   ↑ UP

LARGE

LARGE

MEDIUM

MEDIUM

SMALL

SMALL

MIRRORED for thermal / iron-on transfer
snip along ✂ dotted lines · traditional Chinese throughout

(intentionally blank — back of stencil page)

JAPANESE STYLE	CHINESE STYLE	PRONUNCIATION
(Yuji Boku)	(LXGW WenKai TC)	Mandarin

yīng

On

オウ・ヨウ

Kun

たか

MEANING

eagle, hawk

THE NUANCE

A predator-bird character with 24 strokes. The Chinese
answer to the American eagle - sharp-eyed, far-flying,
alone.

SPOTTED ON

Worn across military, police, and the freedom-seeker
crowd. The in (eagle eye).

HONORARY MENTION

A military, police, and freedom-rider favorite. No
specific named celebrity bearer of solo verified.

WHERE IT GOES

Back, shoulder, full sleeve. This character demands
canvas.

WATCH OUT

Simplified is busier than it looks - either form needs a
tattooist who has done dense Chinese before.

THREE MORE STYLES

yīng · eagle, hawk

BRUSH KAISHO

(Yuji Boku)

ROUNDED HANDWRITING

(Klee One)

TRAD SERIF

(Noto Serif TC)

(verso of explanation · stencil follows)

STENCIL OR TRACE TEMPLATE

yīng · *eagle, hawk*

(Yuji Boku)
JAPANESE STYLE

(LXGW WenKai TC)
CHINESE STYLE

← LEFT

↑ UP

LARGE

LARGE

MEDIUM

MEDIUM

SMALL

SMALL

MIRRORED for thermal / iron-on transfer
snip along ✂ dotted lines · traditional Chinese throughout

(intentionally blank — back of stencil page)

JAPANESE STYLE	CHINESE STYLE	PRONUNCIATION
(Yuji Boku)	(LXGW WenKai TC)	Mandarin

xióng

On
ユウ

Kun
くま

MEANING

bear

THE NUANCE

A big-mammal character with the (fire) radical at the
bottom - the bear was hunted with fire-driven traps.
Strength and steadiness.

SPOTTED ON

Worn by hunters, hikers, and bear-as-personality crowd.
Also a teddy-bear nickname tattoo for some.

HONORARY MENTION

Common among hunters, hikers, and Year-of-the-Bear zodiac
wearers. No specific celebrity bearer documented.

WHERE IT GOES

Shoulder, back, calf. Fits well on a substantial body
part.

WATCH OUT

Don't get confused with (male) - they share components but
mean different things.

THREE MORE STYLES

xióng · bear

BRUSH KAISHO

(Yuji Boku)

ROUNDED HANDWRITING

(Klee One)

TRAD SERIF

(Noto Serif TC)

(verso of explanation · stencil follows)

STENCIL OR TRACE TEMPLATE

xióng · bear

(Yuji Boku)	(LXGW WenKai TC)
← LEFT JAPANESE STYLE	CHINESE STYLE ↑ UP

LARGE

LARGE

MEDIUM

MEDIUM

SMALL

SMALL

MIRRORED for thermal / iron-on transfer
snip along ✂ dotted lines · traditional Chinese throughout

(intentionally blank — back of stencil page)

JAPANESE STYLE	CHINESE STYLE	PRONUNCIATION
(Yuji Boku)	(LXGW WenKai TC)	Mandarin

Mandarin

mǎ

On

バ

Kun

うま・ま

MEANING

horse

THE NUANCE

A pictograph - originally drawn as a side-on horse with mane and four legs. Symbol of speed, freedom, and hard work.

SPOTTED ON

Worn by riders, ranchers, and the Year-of-the-Horse zodiac crowd. Common as a memorial for a beloved animal.

HONORARY MENTION

A Year-of-the-Horse zodiac tattoo and horse-memorial classic. No specific named celebrity bearer documented in press.

WHERE IT GOES

Outer forearm, calf, shoulder. A character that suggests motion.

WATCH OUT

Simplified is - radically different shape. Traditional has 10 strokes and looks like a galloping animal.

THREE MORE STYLES

mǎ · horse

BRUSH KAISHO

(Yuji Boku)

ROUNDED HANDWRITING

(Kiee One)

TRAD SERIF

(Noto Serif TC)

(verso of explanation · stencil follows)

STENCIL OR TRACE TEMPLATE

mǎ · horse

(Yuji Boku)
(LXGW WenKai TC)

← LEFT **JAPANESE STYLE** **CHINESE STYLE** ↑ UP

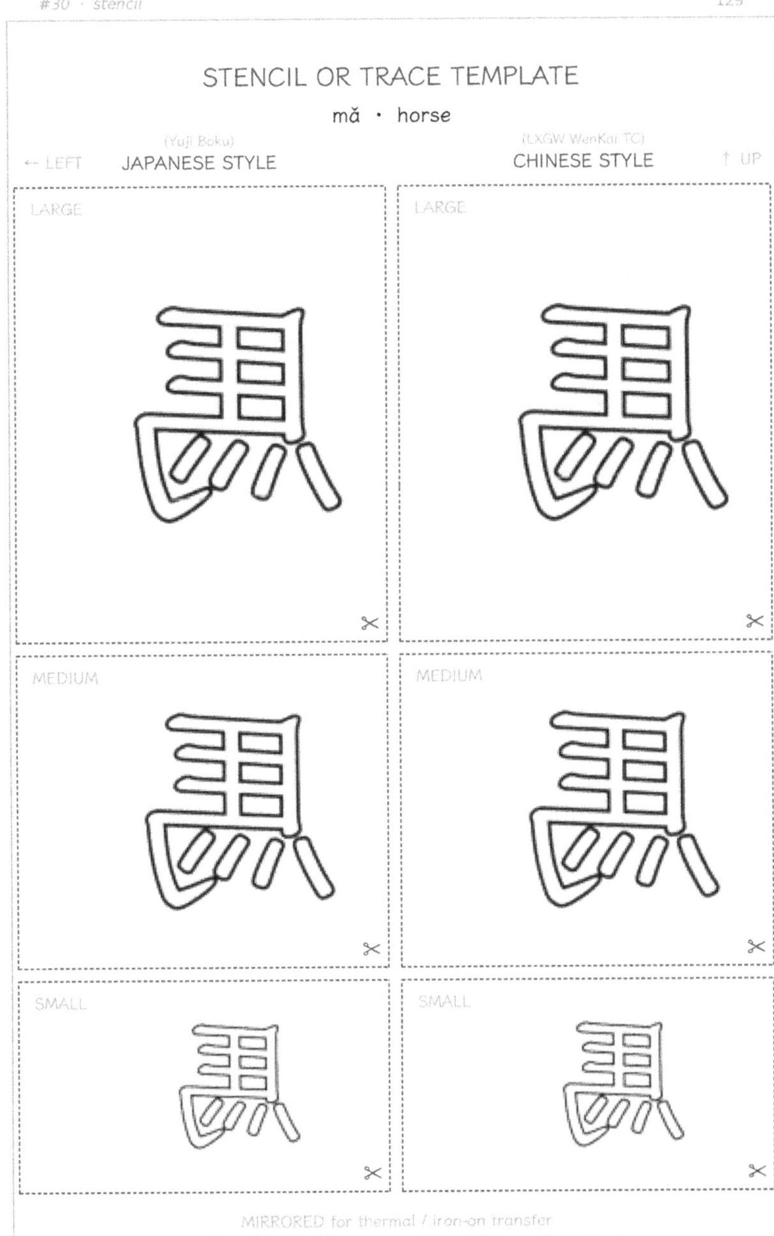

MIRRORED for thermal / iron-on transfer
snip along ✂ dotted lines · traditional Chinese throughout

← LEFT **JAPANESE STYLE** **CHINESE STYLE** ↑ UP

(intentionally blank — back of stencil page)

JAPANESE STYLE
(Yuji Boku)

CHINESE STYLE
(LXGW WenKai TC)

PRONUNCIATION

Mandarin

guǐ

On

キ

Kun

おに

MEANING

ghost, demon, devil

THE NUANCE
Pictograph of a fearsome face with limbs. Not always evil
- in folk religion, includes ancestors and protective
spirits.

SPOTTED ON
Common in horror, metal, and gothic tattoo scenes. Also
worn ironically by people called rascal in their family.

HONORARY MENTION
Common in horror, metal, and gothic tattoo scenes. No
specific named celebrity bearer of solo verified.

WHERE IT GOES
Ribs, calf, back of forearm. A character that wants shadow
placement.

WATCH OUT
Carries a darker tone in modern Mandarin than in classical
- some see it as bad luck. Pick with eyes open.

THREE MORE STYLES

guǐ · *ghost, demon, devil*

BRUSH KAISHO

(Yuji Boku)

ROUNDED HANDWRITING

(Klee One)

TRAD SERIF

(Noto Serif TC)

(verso of explanation · stencil follows)

STENCIL OR TRACE TEMPLATE

guǐ · ghost, demon, devil

(Yuji Boku)
JAPANESE STYLE

(LXGW WenKai TC)
CHINESE STYLE

← LEFT

↑ UP

LARGE

LARGE

MEDIUM

MEDIUM

SMALL

SMALL

← LEFT

JAPANESE STYLE

CHINESE STYLE

↑ UP

(intentionally blank — back of stencil page)

JAPANESE STYLE	CHINESE STYLE	PRONUNCIATION
(Yuji Boku)	(LXGW WenKai TC)	Mandarin

fó

On

ブツ・フツ

Kun

ほとけ

MEANING

Buddha

THE NUANCE

Person radical plus (not) - the awakened one who has gone beyond. Same character used across all Buddhist sects.

SPOTTED ON

Worn across the wellness, yoga, and meditation crowd. Also a respectful nod from non-Buddhists who admire the philosophy.

HONORARY MENTION

Worn across the wellness and meditation crowd though many bearers prefer the simplified from Japanese practice. No specific celebrity bearer of solo verified.

WHERE IT GOES

Back of neck, between shoulder blades, inner forearm. A reverent placement.

WATCH OUT

In some Buddhist traditions, tattooing below the waist is disrespectful. Keep it above the heart.

THREE MORE STYLES

fó · Buddha

BRUSH KAISHO

(Yuji Boku)

ROUNDED HANDWRITING

(Klee One)

TRAD SERIF

(Noto Serif TC)

(verso of explanation · stencil follows)

STENCIL OR TRACE TEMPLATE

fó · Buddha

(Yuji Boku)
JAPANESE STYLE

(LXGW WenKai TC)
CHINESE STYLE

← LEFT

↑ UP

LARGE

LARGE

MEDIUM

MEDIUM

SMALL

SMALL

MIRRORED for thermal / iron-on transfer
snip along ✂ dotted lines · traditional Chinese throughout

(intentionally blank — back of stencil page)

JAPANESE STYLE	CHINESE STYLE	PRONUNCIATION
(Yuji Boku)	(LXGW WenKai TC)	Mandarin

Mandarin

cí

On

ジ

Kun

いつく(しむ)

MEANING

compassion, mercy,

THE NUANCE
Built from over heart - this heart, here, present. The Buddhist virtue of mercy.

SPOTTED ON
Worn by hospice workers, therapists, and the kindness-as-practice crowd.

HONORARY MENTION
Common among hospice workers, therapists, and the kindness-as-practice crowd. No specific named celebrity bearer documented.

WHERE IT GOES
Inner forearm, sternum, between shoulder blades. A soft-energy character.

WATCH OUT
Often confused at small sizes with - confirm the at the bottom is intact.

THREE MORE STYLES

cí · compassion, mercy,

BRUSH KAISHO

(Yuji Boku)

ROUNDED HANDWRITING

(Klee One)

TRAD SERIF

(Noto Serif TC)

(verso of explanation · stencil follows)

STENCIL OR TRACE TEMPLATE

cí · compassion, mercy,

(Yuji Boku)	(LxGW WenKai TC)
← LEFT JAPANESE STYLE	CHINESE STYLE ↑ UP

LARGE

LARGE

MEDIUM

MEDIUM

SMALL

SMALL

MIRRORED for thermal / iron-on transfer
snip along ✂ dotted lines · traditional Chinese throughout

(intentionally blank — back of stencil page)

JAPANESE STYLE	CHINESE STYLE	PRONUNCIATION
(Yuji Boku)	(LXGW WenKai TC)	Mandarin

PRONUNCIATION

Mandarin

zhì

On

チ

Kun

さとし

MEANING

wisdom, intellect

THE NUANCE

Built from (to know) over (sun) - knowing under the sun.
The of Sun Tzu's Art of War - wisdom over force.

SPOTTED ON

Worn by teachers, lawyers, strategists, and self-described
nerds. A gym-bro counterweight tattoo.

HONORARY MENTION

Worn by lawyers, professors, and the
strategy-as-discipline crowd. No specific celebrity bearer
documented.

WHERE IT GOES

Inner forearm, sternum, behind the ear.

WATCH OUT

Don't confuse with alone (just to know) - is the deeper
one with the sun underneath.

THREE MORE STYLES

zhì · wisdom, intellect

BRUSH KAISHO

(Yuji Boku)

ROUNDED HANDWRITING

(Klee One)

TRAD SERIF

(Noto Serif TC)

智

(verso of explanation · stencil follows)

STENCIL OR TRACE TEMPLATE

zhì · wisdom, intellect

(Yuji Boku)
JAPANESE STYLE

(LXGW WenKai TC)
CHINESE STYLE

← LEFT

↑ UP

LARGE

LARGE

MEDIUM

MEDIUM

SMALL

SMALL

MIRRORED for thermal / iron-on transfer
snip along ✂ dotted lines · traditional Chinese throughout

(intentionally blank - back of stencil page)

JAPANESE STYLE
(Yuji Boku)

CHINESE STYLE
(LXGW WenKai TC)

PRONUNCIATION

Mandarin

zhēn

On

シン

Kun

ま・まこと

MEANING

true, real, genuine

THE NUANCE
The character of authenticity. The of (truth) and (sincere heart). No artifice.

SPOTTED ON
Worn solo on wrists across the recovery, sobriety, and authenticity-obsessed crowd. A be-yourself tattoo.

HONORARY MENTION
Common across the recovery and authenticity crowd. No specific celebrity bearer of solo verified.

WHERE IT GOES
Inner wrist, sternum, behind the ear. A center-of-self placement.

WATCH OUT
Looks similar to (straight) - they share top components. Confirm strokes carefully.

THREE MORE STYLES

zhēn · true, real, genuine

BRUSH KAISHO

(Yuji Boku)

ROUNDED HANDWRITING

(Klee One)

TRAD SERIF

(Noto Serif TC)

(verso of explanation · stencil follows)

STENCIL OR TRACE TEMPLATE

zhēn · true, real, genuine

(Yuji Boku)

(LXGW WenKai TC)

JAPANESE STYLE

CHINESE STYLE

LARGE

LARGE

MEDIUM

MEDIUM

SMALL

SMALL

MIRRORED for thermal / iron-on transfer
snip along ✂ dotted lines · traditional Chinese throughout

(intentionally blank — back of stencil page)

JAPANESE STYLE	CHINESE STYLE	PRONUNCIATION
(Yuji Boku)	(LXGW WenKai TC)	Mandarin

Mandarin

shàn

On

ゼン

Kun

よ(い)

MEANING

good, virtuous,

THE NUANCE
The Confucian virtue. Built from sheep over mouth - speak gentle, like a sheep. The of be a good person.

SPOTTED ON
Worn by social workers, teachers, and the do-gooder crowd. Often paired with or .

HONORARY MENTION
Chris 'Birdman' Andersen, NBA, has (good) on the inside of his left forearm and 'evil' on his right got them as his first tattoos at age 21.

WHERE IT GOES
Inner forearm, between shoulder blades, sternum.

WATCH OUT
Has a lecturing energy if worn alone - some prefer to pair with (beauty) for softness.

THREE MORE STYLES

shàn · good, virtuous,

BRUSH KAISHO

(Yuji Boku)

ROUNDED HANDWRITING

(Klee One)

TRAD SERIF

(Noto Serif TC)

(verso of explanation · stencil follows)

STENCIL OR TRACE TEMPLATE

shàn · *good, virtuous,*

(Yuji Boku)
(LXGW WenKai TC)

← LEFT   JAPANESE STYLE   CHINESE STYLE   ↑ UP

MIRRORED for thermal / iron-on transfer
snip along ✂ dotted lines · traditional Chinese throughout

(intentionally blank — back of stencil page)

JAPANESE STYLE	CHINESE STYLE	PRONUNCIATION
(Yuji Boku)	(LXGW WenKai TC)	Mandarin

xìn

On

シン

Kun

—

MEANING

faith, trust, belief

THE NUANCE
Person plus word - a person whose word can be trusted. The root of (credit) and (to trust).

SPOTTED ON
Worn by friends matched in pairs, business partners, and AA-style fellowship members.

HONORARY MENTION
Common as matching tattoos for friends and partners. No specific celebrity bearer of solo documented.

WHERE IT GOES
Inner forearm, sternum, ribs.

WATCH OUT
Lighter than (conviction) - alone is closer to trust than belief. Pick the weight you want.

THREE MORE STYLES

xìn · faith, trust, belief

BRUSH KAISHO

(Yuji Boku)

ROUNDED HANDWRITING

(Klee One)

TRAD SERIF

(Noto Serif TC)

(verso of explanation · stencil follows)

STENCIL OR TRACE TEMPLATE

xìn · faith, trust, belief

(Yuji Boku)
← LEFT JAPANESE STYLE

(LXGW WenKai TC)
CHINESE STYLE ↑ UP

LARGE

LARGE

MEDIUM

MEDIUM

SMALL

SMALL

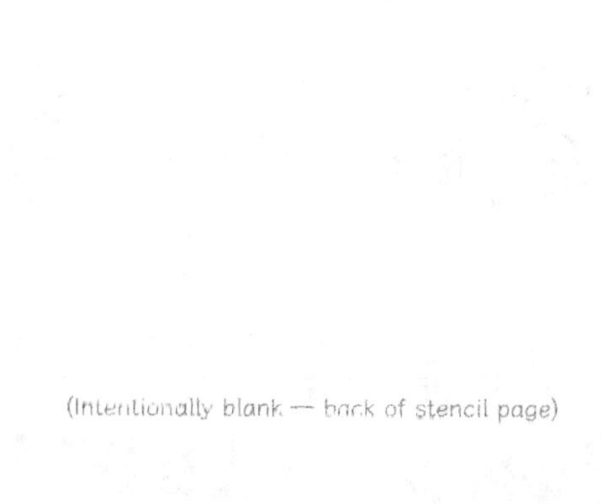

(Intentionally blank — back of stencil page)

JAPANESE STYLE	CHINESE STYLE	PRONUNCIATION
(Yuji Boku)	(LXGW WenKai TC)	Mandarin

dé

On

トク

Kun

—

MEANING

virtue, ethics,

THE NUANCE
The of (morality, Tao+virtue). Step radical plus (straight) plus (heart) - walk straight from the heart.

SPOTTED ON
Worn by Confucian scholars, ethics professors, and serious-minded teens looking for gravitas.

HONORARY MENTION
A Confucian-virtue tattoo for ethics professors and serious-minded teens. No specific celebrity bearer documented.

WHERE IT GOES
Between shoulder blades, sternum, inner forearm.

WATCH OUT
15 strokes - dense. Make sure your tattooist has done complex Chinese before.

THREE MORE STYLES

dé · virtue, ethics,

BRUSH KAISHO

(Yuji Boku)

ROUNDED HANDWRITING

(Klee One)

TRAD SERIF

(Noto Serif TC)

(verso of explanation · stencil follows)

STENCIL OR TRACE TEMPLATE

dé · virtue, ethics,

(Yuji Boku)
← LEFT   JAPANESE STYLE

(LXGW WenKai TC)
CHINESE STYLE   ↑ UP

LARGE

LARGE

MEDIUM

MEDIUM

SMALL

SMALL

(intentionally blank — back of stencil page)

JAPANESE STYLE	CHINESE STYLE	PRONUNCIATION
(Yuji Boku)	(LXGW WenKai TC)	Mandarin

Mandarin
zhōng

On
チュウ

Kun
—

MEANING

loyalty,

THE NUANCE
Built from middle over heart - heart in the right place,
dead center. Allen Iverson famously had this on his neck.

SPOTTED ON
Common in NBA and NFL locker rooms. Also worn by veterans,
brothers, and members of long-running crews.

HONORARY MENTION
Allen Iverson, Philadelphia 76ers, has (loyalty) tattooed
on the right side of his neck. Single most-cited example
of the character in NBA history.

WHERE IT GOES
Neck, sternum, inner bicep.

WATCH OUT
Pairs powerfully with (honor) - was the motto of countless
wuxia heroes.

THREE MORE STYLES

zhōng · loyalty,

BRUSH KAISHO

(Yuji Boku)

ROUNDED HANDWRITING

(Klee One)

TRAD SERIF

(Noto Serif TC)

(verso of explanation · stencil follows)

STENCIL OR TRACE TEMPLATE

zhōng · loyalty,

(Yuji Boku)
JAPANESE STYLE

(LXGW WenKai TC)
CHINESE STYLE

← LEFT

↑ UP

MIRRORED for thermal / iron-on transfer
snip along ✂ dotted lines · traditional Chinese throughout

(intentionally blank — back of stencil page)

JAPANESE STYLE	CHINESE STYLE	PRONUNCIATION
(Yuji Boku)	(LXGW WenKai TC)	Mandarin

Mandarin

lè

On

ガク・ラク

Kun

たの(しい)

MEANING

joy, happiness;

THE NUANCE
Pictograph of a wooden frame with two silk strings -
originally meant musical instrument, then music, then joy.

SPOTTED ON
Worn by musicians (read as yuè), artists, and the
joy-as-discipline crowd (read as lè).

HONORARY MENTION
Common among musicians (read yuè) and the joy-as-practice
crowd (read lè). No specific celebrity bearer of solo
verified.

WHERE IT GOES
Inner forearm, ribcage, behind the ear.

WATCH OUT
Two readings depending on meaning. If you want music, the
pinyin is yuè; if joy, it's lè. Same character either way.

THREE MORE STYLES

lè · joy, happiness;

BRUSH KAISHO

(Yuji Boku)

ROUNDED HANDWRITING

(Klee One)

TRAD SERIF

(Noto Serif TC)

(verso of explanation · stencil follows)

STENCIL OR TRACE TEMPLATE

lè · *joy, happiness;*

JAPANESE STYLE	CHINESE STYLE
LARGE 	LARGE 
MEDIUM 	MEDIUM 
SMALL 	SMALL 

MIRRORED for thermal / iron-on transfer
snip along ✂ dotted lines · traditional Chinese throughout

(Intentionally blank — back of stencil page)

JAPANESE STYLE	CHINESE STYLE	PRONUNCIATION
(Yuji Boku)	(LXGW WenKai TC)	Mandarin

jìng

On

セイ・ジョウ

Kun

しず(か)

MEANING

quiet, stillness,

THE NUANCE
Built from blue/green plus (to contend) - the stillness
AFTER the fight. Earned calm, not absent calm.

SPOTTED ON
Worn across the meditation, therapy, and recovery crowd. A
favorite among introverts and post-burnout types.

HONORARY MENTION
Common across the meditation, therapy, and post-burnout
tattoo crowd. No specific celebrity bearer documented.

WHERE IT GOES
Inner forearm, sternum, between shoulder blades. Quiet
placements for a quiet character.

WATCH OUT
Simplified loses the right-side complexity. Traditional is
the meditator's pick.

THREE MORE STYLES

jìng · quiet, stillness,

BRUSH KAISHO

(Yuji Boku)

ROUNDED HANDWRITING

(Klee One)

TRAD SERIF

(Noto Serif TC)

(verso of explanation · stencil follows)

STENCIL OR TRACE TEMPLATE

jìng · quiet, stillness,

(Yuji Boku)
JAPANESE STYLE

(LXGW WenKai TC)
CHINESE STYLE

← LEFT

↑ UP

LARGE

LARGE

MEDIUM

MEDIUM

SMALL

SMALL

MIRRORED for thermal / iron-on transfer
snip along ✂ dotted lines · traditional Chinese throughout

(intentionally blank — back of stencil page)

JAPANESE STYLE	CHINESE STYLE	PRONUNCIATION
(Yuji Boku)	(LXGW WenKai TC)	Mandarin

PRONUNCIATION

Mandarin

ān

On

アン

Kun

やす(い)

MEANING

peace, safe, secure

THE NUANCE
Built from roof over woman - a woman under a roof, safe at home. The of (peace) and (safety).

SPOTTED ON
Common pick after a hard year - illness, divorce, recovery. A bedside-table tattoo.

HONORARY MENTION
Common after illness, divorce, or recovery a bedside-table tattoo. No specific celebrity bearer documented in press.

WHERE IT GOES
Inner wrist, sternum, behind the ear. A soft-skin character.

WATCH OUT
The character originated in agrarian China - some modern readers find the woman-under-roof image dated. Decide for yourself.

THREE MORE STYLES

ān · peace, safe, secure

BRUSH KAISHO

(Yuji Boku)

ROUNDED HANDWRITING

(Klee One)

TRAD SERIF

(Noto Serif TC)

(verso of explanation · stencil follows)

STENCIL OR TRACE TEMPLATE

ān • *peace, safe, secure*

(Yuji Boku)   (LXGW WenKai TC)

← LEFT   **JAPANESE STYLE**   **CHINESE STYLE**   ↑ UP

LARGE

LARGE

MEDIUM

MEDIUM

SMALL

SMALL

MIRRORED for thermal / iron-on transfer
snip along ✂ dotted lines · traditional Chinese throughout

(intentionally blank — back of stencil page)

JAPANESE STYLE	CHINESE STYLE	PRONUNCIATION

(Yuji Boku) (LXGW WenKai TC) Mandarin

mìng

On

メイ・ミョウ

Kun

いのち

MEANING

life, fate, destiny

THE NUANCE
Means both biological life AND the bigger arc of fate. The
of (revolution) and (life).

SPOTTED ON
Worn after near-death experiences, big diagnoses, or
pivotal years. A stamped-by-fate character.

HONORARY MENTION
David Beckham's torso proverb contains the character of
life-and-fate lives at the start of the line. He has
discussed the tattoo with Asia Society.

WHERE IT GOES
Sternum, ribs, inner forearm.

WATCH OUT
Heavy character - not a casual pick. People will assume
there's a story.

THREE MORE STYLES

mìng · life, fate, destiny

BRUSH KAISHO

(Yuji Boku)

ROUNDED HANDWRITING

(Klee One)

TRAD SERIF

(Noto Serif TC)

(verso of explanation · stencil follows)

STENCIL OR TRACE TEMPLATE

mìng · life, fate, destiny

(Yuji Boku)
JAPANESE STYLE

(LXGW WenKai TC)
CHINESE STYLE

LARGE

LARGE

MEDIUM

MEDIUM

SMALL

SMALL

MIRRORED for thermal / iron on transfer
snip along ✂ dotted lines · traditional Chinese throughout

← LEFT   JAPANESE STYLE   CHINESE STYLE   ↑ UP

(intentionally blank - back of stencil page)

JAPANESE STYLE	CHINESE STYLE	PRONUNCIATION
(Yuji Boku)	(LXGW WenKai TC)	Mandarin

Mandarin

hún

On

コン

Kun

たましい

MEANING

soul, spirit

THE NUANCE
Built from cloud plus ghost - the cloud-ghost, the part
that floats free. In Chinese folk thought, the soul that
wanders.

SPOTTED ON
Worn by musicians, artists, and the soul-music aesthetic
crowd. Also a memorial-tattoo classic.

HONORARY MENTION
Common among musicians, artists, and the soul-music
aesthetic crowd. No specific celebrity bearer of solo
verified.

WHERE IT GOES
Sternum, between shoulder blades, inner forearm. A
center-of-being placement.

WATCH OUT
Has a slightly mystical/folk-religion flavor - heavier
than (heart). Pick the weight you want.

THREE MORE STYLES

hún · soul, spirit

BRUSH KAISHO

(Yuji Boku)

ROUNDED HANDWRITING

(Klee One)

TRAD SERIF

(Noto Serif TC)

(verso of explanation · stencil follows)

STENCIL OR TRACE TEMPLATE

hún · soul, spirit

(Yuji Boku)
JAPANESE STYLE

(LXGW WenKai TC)
CHINESE STYLE

← LEFT

↑ UP

LARGE

LARGE

MEDIUM

MEDIUM

SMALL

SMALL

MIRRORED for thermal / iron-on transfer
snip along ✂ dotted lines · traditional Chinese throughout

(intentionally blank — back of stencil page)

JAPANESE STYLE	CHINESE STYLE	PRONUNCIATION
(Yuji Boku)	(LXGW WenKai TC)	Mandarin

fēi

On

ヒ

Kun

と(ぶ)・と(ばす)

MEANING

to fly, soar

THE NUANCE

Pictograph of a bird in flight - wings spread, tail trailing. The of pilots, dancers, and dreamers.

SPOTTED ON

Worn by aviators, dancers, athletes, and the take-off-already crowd. Common as part of larger nature pieces.

HONORARY MENTION

Common among aviators and dancers. No specific named celebrity bearer of solo documented.

WHERE IT GOES

Outer forearm, calf, shoulder blade. A character with motion - place it where it can move.

WATCH OUT

Simplified is - half the strokes. Traditional actually looks like wings; simplified looks like a checkmark.

THREE MORE STYLES

fēi · to fly, soar

BRUSH KAISHO

(Yuji Boku)

ROUNDED HANDWRITING

(Kiee One)

TRAD SERIF

(Noto Serif TC)

STENCIL OR TRACE TEMPLATE

fēi · to fly, soar

(Yuji Boku)	(LXGW WenKai TC)
← LEFT JAPANESE STYLE	CHINESE STYLE ↑ UP

LARGE

LARGE

MEDIUM

MEDIUM

SMALL

SMALL

MIRRORED for thermal / iron-on transfer
snip along ✂ dotted lines · traditional Chinese throughout

(intentionally blank — back of stencil page)

JAPANESE STYLE	CHINESE STYLE	PRONUNCIATION
(Yuji Boku)	(LXGW WenKai TC)	Mandarin

PRONUNCIATION

Mandarin
zhàn

On
セン

Kun
いくさ・たたか(う)

MEANING

battle, war, fight

THE NUANCE
Built from single plus spear - one warrior with a spear.
The of (warrior) and (war).

SPOTTED ON
Worn by veterans, fighters, and anyone who has been
through a serious season of conflict.

HONORARY MENTION
Common among veterans and post-conflict tattoo wearers. No
single named celebrity bearer of solo verified though
every UFC walkout features it somewhere.

WHERE IT GOES
Bicep, chest, ribs.

WATCH OUT
Heavier than - is the discipline, is the actual fight.
Pick deliberately.

THREE MORE STYLES

zhàn · battle, war, fight

BRUSH KAISHO

(Yuji Boku)

ROUNDED HANDWRITING

(Klee One)

TRAD SERIF

(Noto Serif TC)

(verso of explanation · stencil follows)

STENCIL OR TRACE TEMPLATE

zhàn · battle, war, fight

(Yuji Boku)
← LEFT   JAPANESE STYLE

(LXGW WenKai TC)
CHINESE STYLE   ↑ UP

LARGE

LARGE

MEDIUM

MEDIUM

SMALL

SMALL

(intentionally blank — back of stencil page)

JAPANESE STYLE	CHINESE STYLE	PRONUNCIATION
(Yuji Boku)	(LXGW WenKai TC)	Mandarin

wáng

On

オウ

Kun

—

MEANING

king, monarch

THE NUANCE

Three horizontal strokes connected by a vertical - heaven, earth, humanity united by the ruler. Confucian, regal, and zero subtlety.

SPOTTED ON

Worn across hip-hop, NBA, and chess subcultures. LeBron-tier energy.

HONORARY MENTION

Worn across hip-hop and chess subcultures with LeBron-tier energy. No specific celebrity bearer of solo verified in mainstream press.

WHERE IT GOES

Forearm, neck, sternum. A character that wants visibility.

WATCH OUT

Carries a bragging tone - some Chinese speakers find it self-congratulatory worn solo. Be ready to own it.

THREE MORE STYLES

wáng · king, monarch

BRUSH KAISHO

(Yuji Boku)

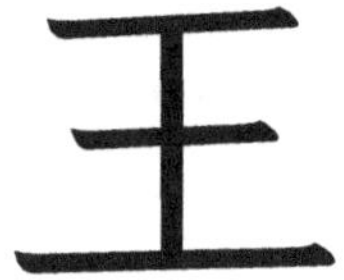

ROUNDED HANDWRITING

(Klee One)

TRAD SERIF

(Noto Serif TC)

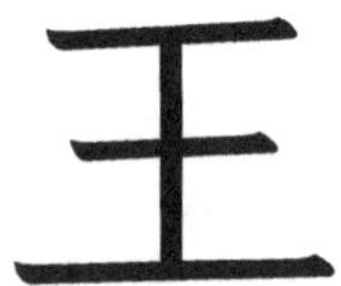

(verso of explanation · stencil follows)

STENCIL OR TRACE TEMPLATE

wáng · king, monarch

(Yuji Boku)
JAPANESE STYLE

(LXGW WenKai TC)
CHINESE STYLE

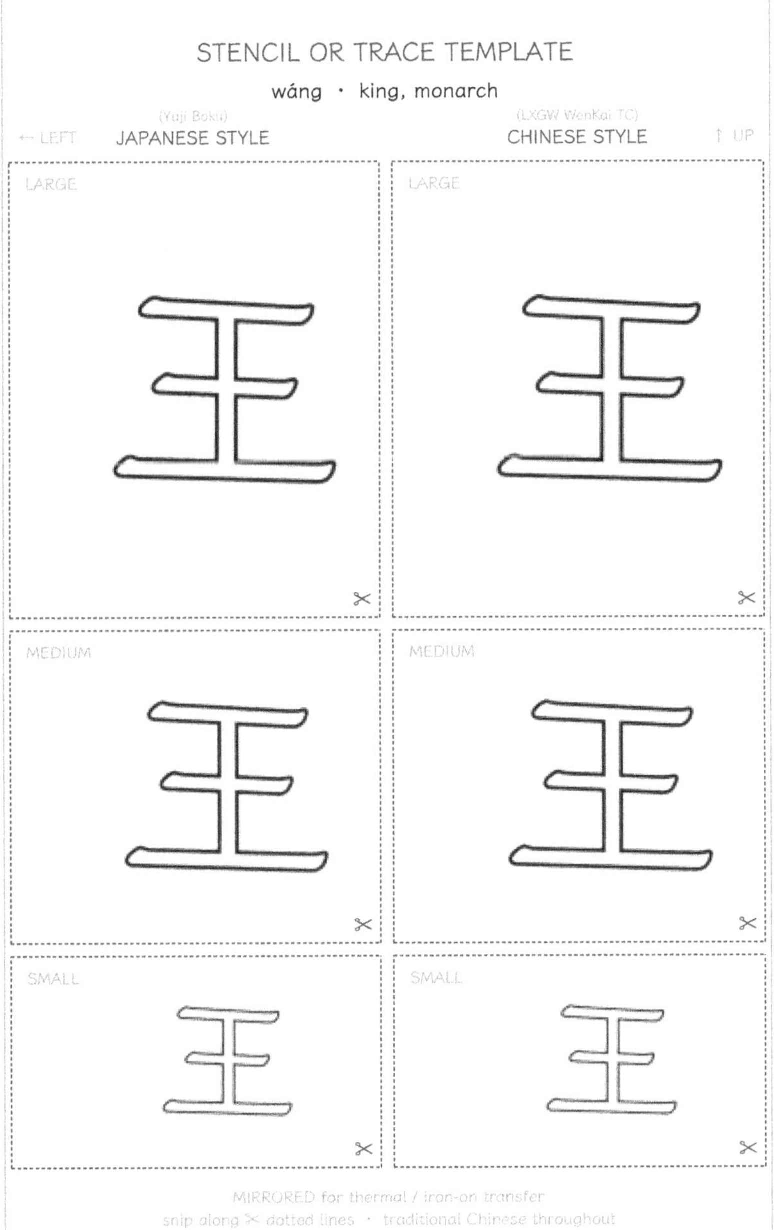

(intentionally blank — back of stencil page)

JAPANESE STYLE	CHINESE STYLE	PRONUNCIATION
(Yuji Boku)	(LXGW WenKai TC)	Mandarin

PRONUNCIATION

Mandarin

xuě

On

セツ

Kun

ゆき

MEANING

snow

THE NUANCE

Built from rain plus broom radical - rain you can sweep.
Pure, cold, quiet. Six-pointed pictograph in early forms.

SPOTTED ON

Worn by skiers, snowboarders, and the Nordic-aesthetic
crowd. Also a name-tattoo for anyone called Snow or Yuki.

HONORARY MENTION

A Year-of-the-Snake-adjacent tattoo and a name tattoo for
those called Snow or Yuki. No specific celebrity bearer
documented.

WHERE IT GOES

Inner wrist, behind the ear, ankle. A delicate placement.

WATCH OUT

Often paired with (mountain) for snow-capped imagery.
Combined as reads as snowy mountain.

THREE MORE STYLES

xuě · snow

BRUSH KAISHO

(Yuji Boku)

ROUNDED HANDWRITING

(Klee One)

TRAD SERIF

(Noto Serif TC)

(verso of explanation · stencil follows)

STENCIL OR TRACE TEMPLATE

xuě · snow

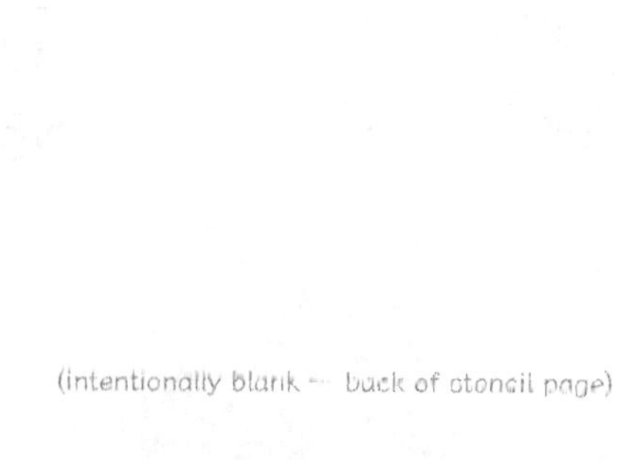
(intentionally blank — back of stencil page)

JAPANESE STYLE	CHINESE STYLE	PRONUNCIATION
(Yuji Boku)	(LXGW WenKai TC)	Mandarin

yǐng

On
エイ

Kun
かげ

MEANING

shadow

THE NUANCE
Built from (scene/light) plus three slanted strokes - the slanted ghost of the light. The of cinema and silhouettes.

SPOTTED ON
Worn by photographers, filmmakers, and the shadow-self psychology crowd.

HONORARY MENTION
Worn by photographers, filmmakers, and the shadow-self psychology crowd. No specific celebrity bearer documented.

WHERE IT GOES
Outer forearm, calf, ribs. A moody placement.

WATCH OUT
At small sizes the right-side can blur into nothing. Don't go too tiny.

THREE MORE STYLES

yǐng · shadow

BRUSH KAISHO

(Yuji Boku)

ROUNDED HANDWRITING

(Klee One)

TRAD SERIF

(Noto Serif TC)

STENCIL OR TRACE TEMPLATE

yǐng · shadow

(Yuji Boku)
← LEFT **JAPANESE STYLE**

(LXGW WenKai TC)
CHINESE STYLE ↑ UP

LARGE

LARGE

MEDIUM

MEDIUM

SMALL

SMALL

(intentionally blank — back of stencil page)

JAPANESE STYLE	CHINESE STYLE	PRONUNCIATION
(Yuji Boku)	(LXGW WenKai TC)	Mandarin

guāng

On
コウ

Kun
ひかり・ひか(る)

MEANING

light, ray, glory

THE NUANCE
Pictograph of a person holding a torch above their head.
The of (sunlight) and (glory).

SPOTTED ON
Common after dark seasons - mental health recoveries,
post-rehab, end-of-grief tattoos.

HONORARY MENTION
Common after dark seasons mental health recoveries,
post-rehab. No specific celebrity bearer of solo verified.

WHERE IT GOES
Inner forearm, sternum, behind the ear.

WATCH OUT
Pairs visually with (shadow) - couples or close friends
sometimes split the pair across two bodies.

THREE MORE STYLES

guāng · light, ray, glory

BRUSH KAISHO

(Yuji Boku)

ROUNDED HANDWRITING

(Klee One)

TRAD SERIF

(Noto Serif TC)

(verso of explanation · stencil follows)

STENCIL OR TRACE TEMPLATE

guāng · light, ray, glory

← LEFT	(Yuji Boku) JAPANESE STYLE	(LXGW WenKai TC) CHINESE STYLE	↑ UP

LARGE

LARGE

MEDIUM

MEDIUM

SMALL

SMALL

← LEFT   JAPANESE STYLE   CHINESE STYLE   ↑ UP

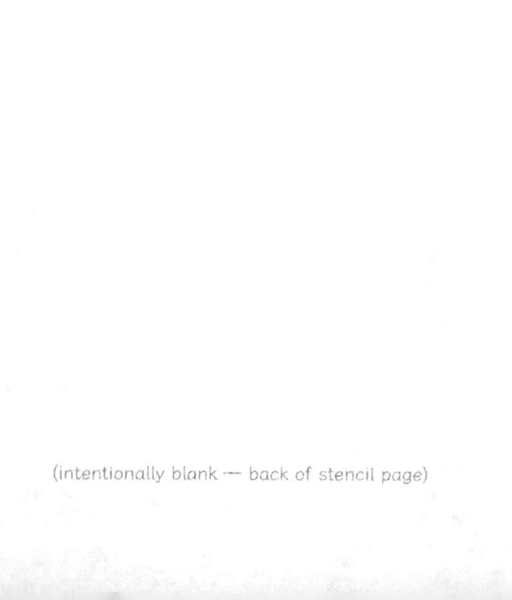

(intentionally blank -- back of stencil page)

<table>
<tr><td>

JAPANESE STYLE

(Yuji Boku)

</td><td>

CHINESE STYLE

(LXGW WenKai TC)

</td><td>

PRONUNCIATION

Mandarin

léi

On

ライ

Kun

かみなり

MEANING

thunder</td></tr>
</table>

THE NUANCE

Built from rain plus field - rain over the field, the boom
that comes with the storm. Sudden, loud, decisive.

SPOTTED ON

Worn by drummers, bikers, and the storm-chaser crowd. Also
the in Marvel's Thor ( ) translations.

HONORARY MENTION

Common among drummers, bikers, and the storm-chaser crowd.
No specific named celebrity bearer of solo verified.

WHERE IT GOES

Bicep, chest, calf. A loud-energy placement.

WATCH OUT

Don't pair with cute imagery - is hammer-of-the-gods
volume.

THREE MORE STYLES

léi · thunder

BRUSH KAISHO

(Yuji Boku)

ROUNDED HANDWRITING

(Klee One)

TRAD SERIF

(Noto Serif TC)

STENCIL OR TRACE TEMPLATE

léi · thunder

(intentionally blank — back of stencil page)

JAPANESE STYLE	CHINESE STYLE	PRONUNCIATION
(Yuji Boku)	(LXGW WenKai TC)	Mandarin

Mandarin
shé

On
ジャ・ダ

Kun
へび

MEANING

snake, serpent

THE NUANCE
Insect/reptile radical plus (it). Symbol of cunning, transformation, and patience in Chinese culture - not the Western devil.

SPOTTED ON
Year of the Snake zodiac tattoo. Also worn across the wellness/medicine crowd (caduceus parallel).

HONORARY MENTION
A Year-of-the-Snake zodiac tattoo classic. No specific celebrity bearer of solo documented.

WHERE IT GOES
Forearm wrap, calf, neck. A character that suggests coiling.

WATCH OUT
In Chinese folklore, the snake is mostly positive - don't assume Western Eden symbolism.

THREE MORE STYLES

shé · snake, serpent

BRUSH KAISHO

(Yuji Boku)

ROUNDED HANDWRITING

(Klee One)

TRAD SERIF

(Noto Serif TC)

STENCIL OR TRACE TEMPLATE
shé · snake, serpent

(Yuji Boku)   (LXGW WenKai TC)

← LEFT   **JAPANESE STYLE**   **CHINESE STYLE**   ↑ UP

LARGE   LARGE

MEDIUM   MEDIUM

SMALL   SMALL

MIRRORED for thermal / iron-on transfer
snip along ✂ dotted lines · traditional Chinese throughout

(intentionally blank — back of stencil page)

JAPANESE STYLE	CHINESE STYLE	PRONUNCIATION
(Yuji Boku)	(LXGW WenKai TC)	Mandarin

Mandarin

xiào

On

ショウ

Kun

わら(う)・え(む)

MEANING

smile, laugh

THE NUANCE

Bamboo radical over (young) - bamboo bending in the wind looks like laughter. Light, airy, never heavy.

SPOTTED ON

Worn solo on wrists across the joy-as-rebellion crowd. Often paired with for double joy.

HONORARY MENTION

Common in the joy-as-rebellion tattoo crowd. No specific celebrity bearer of solo documented.

WHERE IT GOES

Inner wrist, behind the ear, ankle.

WATCH OUT

The character literally means smile/laugh - it does NOT mean happy or fun in general. Pick precisely.

THREE MORE STYLES

xiào · smile, laugh

BRUSH KAISHO

(Yuji Boku)

ROUNDED HANDWRITING

(Klee One)

TRAD SERIF

(Noto Serif TC)

(verso of explanation · stencil follows)

STENCIL OR TRACE TEMPLATE

xiào · smile, laugh

(Yuji Boku)
JAPANESE STYLE

(LXGW WenKai TC)
CHINESE STYLE

← LEFT

↑ UP

LARGE

LARGE

MEDIUM

MEDIUM

SMALL

SMALL

MIRRORED for thermal / iron-on transfer
snip along ✂ dotted lines · traditional Chinese throughout

JAPANESE STYLE	CHINESE STYLE	PRONUNCIATION
(Yuji Boku)	(LXGW WenKai TC)	Mandarin

雅　雅

yǎ

On
カ

Kun
みやび

MEANING

elegant, refined,

THE NUANCE
Built from (tooth) plus (small bird) - the small bird's
tooth, fine and precise. The of high culture.

SPOTTED ON
Worn by designers, architects, dancers, and anyone
aspiring to taste-as-discipline.

HONORARY MENTION
Common in design, dance, and architecture worlds. No
specific celebrity bearer of solo verified.

WHERE IT GOES
Inner forearm, behind the ear, ankle. A discreet placement
for a discreet character.

WATCH OUT
Slightly feminine connotation in modern usage - though
plenty of men wear it. Decide for yourself.

THREE MORE STYLES

yǎ · elegant, refined,

BRUSH KAISHO

(Yuji Boku)

ROUNDED HANDWRITING

(Klee One)

TRAD SERIF

(Noto Serif TC)

(verso of explanation · stencil follows)

STENCIL OR TRACE TEMPLATE
yǎ · elegant, refined,

LARGE

LARGE

MEDIUM

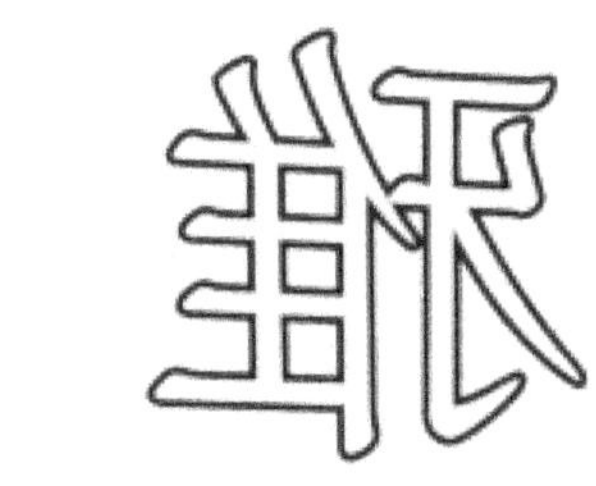

MEDIUM

SMALL

SMALL

(intentionally blank — back of stencil page)

JAPANESE STYLE	CHINESE STYLE	PRONUNCIATION
(Yuji Boku)	(LXGW WenKai TC)	Mandarin

yún

On

ウン

Kun

くも

MEANING

cloud

THE NUANCE
Pictograph of swirling vapor under the rain radical . The
of mountain-and-cloud landscape paintings.

SPOTTED ON
Worn by pilots, hikers, and the daydreamer crowd. Often
paired with or .

HONORARY MENTION
Common among pilots and the daydreamer crowd. No specific
celebrity bearer of solo documented.

WHERE IT GOES
Sternum, between shoulder blades, ribs. A drifting
placement.

WATCH OUT
Simplified is a dramatic reduction - just the swirl, no
rain. Traditional has more atmosphere.

THREE MORE STYLES

yún · cloud

BRUSH KAISHO

(Yuji Boku)

ROUNDED HANDWRITING

(Klee One)

TRAD SERIF

(Noto Serif TC)

STENCIL OR TRACE TEMPLATE
yún · cloud

(Yuji Boku)	(LXGW WenKai TC)
← LEFT JAPANESE STYLE	CHINESE STYLE ↑ UP

LARGE

LARGE

MEDIUM

MEDIUM

SMALL

SMALL

(intentionally blank — back of stencil page)

JAPANESE STYLE	CHINESE STYLE	PRONUNCIATION
(Yuji Boku)	(LXGW WenKai TC)	Mandarin

huā

On

カ・ケ

Kun

はな

MEANING

flower

THE NUANCE
Grass radical plus (to transform). Beauty as transformation. The of cherry blossoms and impermanence.

SPOTTED ON
A common name-tattoo (countless people called Flower or Hana). Also a tattoo for new beginnings and recoveries.

HONORARY MENTION
A common name-tattoo for those called Hana, Flora, or Flower. No specific celebrity bearer of solo verified.

WHERE IT GOES
Inner wrist, behind the ear, ankle, ribs.

WATCH OUT
Pairs with names or other softer characters. Combined with reads as beautiful flower.

THREE MORE STYLES

huā · flower

BRUSH KAISHO

(Yuji Boku)

ROUNDED HANDWRITING

(Klee One)

TRAD SERIF

(Noto Serif TC)

(verso of explanation · stencil follows)

STENCIL OR TRACE TEMPLATE

huā · flower

(Yuji Boku)	(LXGW WenKai TC)
JAPANESE STYLE	CHINESE STYLE

← LEFT   ↑ UP

LARGE

LARGE

MEDIUM

MEDIUM

SMALL

SMALL

MIRRORED for thermal / iron-on transfer
snip along ✂ dotted lines · traditional Chinese throughout

(intentionally blank — back of stencil page)

JAPANESE STYLE	CHINESE STYLE	PRONUNCIATION
(Yuji Boku)	(LXGW WenKai TC)	Mandarin

xiáng

On

ショウ

Kun

かけ(る)

MEANING

to soar, hover

THE NUANCE
Built from (sheep) over wing-feather radical - though the sheep here is phonetic, not literal. Means to fly with extended wings.

SPOTTED ON
Worn by pilots, dancers, and the soar-not-just-fly crowd. The of athletic names.

HONORARY MENTION
A pilot, dancer, and athletic-name tattoo. No specific celebrity bearer of solo documented.

WHERE IT GOES
Outer forearm, calf, shoulder blade.

WATCH OUT
Less common than (to fly) - implies sustained gliding. Pick the verb you mean.

THREE MORE STYLES

xiáng · to soar, hover

BRUSH KAISHO

(Yuji Boku)

ROUNDED HANDWRITING

(Klee One)

TRAD SERIF

(Noto Serif TC)

STENCIL OR TRACE TEMPLATE

xiáng · to soar, hover

(Yuji Boku)
JAPANESE STYLE

(LXGW WenKai TC)
CHINESE STYLE

LARGE

LARGE

MEDIUM

MEDIUM

SMALL

SMALL

(intentionally blank — back of stencil page)

JAPANESE STYLE	CHINESE STYLE	PRONUNCIATION

JAPANESE STYLE
(Yuji Boku)

CHINESE STYLE
(LXGW WenKai TC)

PRONUNCIATION

Mandarin

nù

On

ド

Kun

いか(る)・おこ(る)

MEANING

anger, fury, wrath

THE NUANCE
Built from slave over heart - the enslaved heart that
bursts. Real anger, the kind that means it.

SPOTTED ON
Worn by drummers, fighters, and the rage-as-fuel crowd.
Also seen ironically on the perpetually-chill.

HONORARY MENTION
Common in metal and drumming scenes. No specific celebrity
bearer of solo documented (most bearers don't advertise
this one).

WHERE IT GOES
Bicep, chest, ribs.

WATCH OUT
Don't tattoo lightly - it reads as a confession, not a
warning. Some Chinese speakers see it as a red flag.

THREE MORE STYLES

nù · anger, fury, wrath

BRUSH KAISHO

(Yuji Boku)

ROUNDED HANDWRITING

(Klee One)

TRAD SERIF

(Noto Serif TC)

(verso of explanation · stencil follows)

STENCIL OR TRACE TEMPLATE

nù · anger, fury, wrath

(Yuji Boku)
← LEFT   JAPANESE STYLE

(LXGW WenKai TC)
CHINESE STYLE   ↑ UP

LARGE

LARGE

MEDIUM

MEDIUM

SMALL

SMALL

MIRRORED for thermal / iron-on transfer
snip along ✂ dotted lines · traditional Chinese throughout

(intentionally blank — back of stencil page)

JAPANESE STYLE	CHINESE STYLE	PRONUNCIATION
(Yuji Boku)	(LXGW WenKai TC)	Mandarin

PRONUNCIATION

Mandarin

xǐng

On

セイ

Kun

さ(める)・さ(ます)

MEANING

to wake up, awaken,

THE NUANCE

Wine radical plus star - sobered up under the morning star. Both literal waking and metaphorical awakening.

SPOTTED ON

A staple in the recovery and sobriety community. Also worn by those who came out of long fogs.

HONORARY MENTION

A staple in the recovery and sobriety community. No specific celebrity bearer of solo documented in mainstream press.

WHERE IT GOES

Inner forearm, sternum, between shoulder blades.

WATCH OUT

More precise than (jué, to perceive/awaken). specifically implies coming OUT of sleep or stupor.

THREE MORE STYLES

xǐng · to wake up, awaken,

BRUSH KAISHO

(Yuji Boku)

ROUNDED HANDWRITING

(Klee One)

TRAD SERIF

(Noto Serif TC)

STENCIL OR TRACE TEMPLATE

xǐng · to wake up, awaken,

(Yuji Boku)

(LXGW WenKai TC)

← LEFT   **JAPANESE STYLE**   **CHINESE STYLE**   ↑ UP

LARGE

LARGE

MEDIUM

MEDIUM

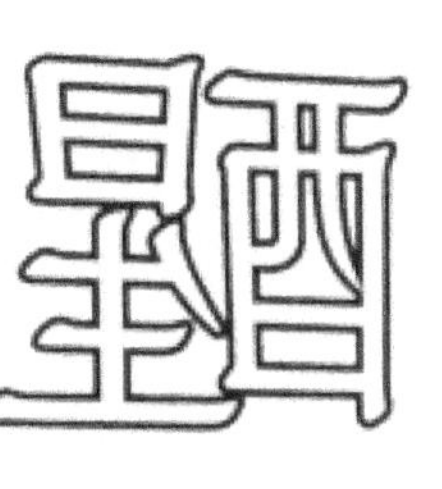

SMALL

SMALL

(intentionally blank — back of stencil page)

JAPANESE STYLE	CHINESE STYLE	PRONUNCIATION
(Yuji Boku)	(LXGW WenKai TC)	Mandarin

jìng

On

キョウ

Kun

かがみ

MEANING

mirror

THE NUANCE

Metal radical plus (eventually) - the polished metal that finally shows you to yourself. A self-reflection character.

SPOTTED ON

Worn across the therapy, journaling, and self-examination crowd. Also a stage-magic-aesthetic tattoo.

HONORARY MENTION

Worn across the therapy and journaling tattoo crowd. No specific celebrity bearer of solo documented.

WHERE IT GOES

Sternum, inner forearm, behind the ear.

WATCH OUT

19 strokes in traditional. A precise tattooist is required - sloppy strokes turn into a smudge.

THREE MORE STYLES

jìng · mirror

BRUSH KAISHO

(Yuji Boku)

ROUNDED HANDWRITING

(Klee One)

TRAD SERIF

(Noto Serif TC)

STENCIL OR TRACE TEMPLATE

jìng · mirror

(Yuji Boku)
JAPANESE STYLE

(LXGW WenKai TC)
CHINESE STYLE

LARGE

LARGE

MEDIUM

MEDIUM

SMALL

SMALL

MIRRORED for thermal / iron-on transfer
snip along ✂ dotted lines · traditional Chinese throughout

(intentionally blank — back of stencil page)

Part II · Short Phrases

twenty two-character classics

(intentionally blank — back of stencil page)

JAPANESE STYLE	CHINESE STYLE	PRONUNCIATION
(Yuji Boku)	(LXGW WenKai TC)	Mandarin

zì yóu

On

ジ / ユウ

Kun

みずか(ら) / ―

MEANING

freedom, liberty

THE NUANCE

Two characters: self and from-cause . Literally from-self
- to act from oneself.

SPOTTED ON

Worn by activists, expats, anyone who has left a place to
find themselves. A rebel-yell phrase.

HONORARY MENTION

Common across activists, expats, and the rebel-yell tattoo
crowd. No specific celebrity bearer of as a phrase
verified in press.

WHERE IT GOES

Spine (vertical), forearm (horizontal), ribs.

WATCH OUT

Vertical reading goes top-to-bottom: above .

THREE MORE STYLES

zì yóu · freedom, liberty

BRUSH KAISHO

(Yuji Boku)

ROUNDED HANDWRITING

(Klee One)

TRAD SERIF

(Noto Serif TC)

(verso of explanation · stencil follows)

STENCIL OR TRACE TEMPLATE

zì yóu · freedom, liberty

(intentionally blank — back of stencil page)

JAPANESE STYLE	CHINESE STYLE	PRONUNCIATION
(Yuji Boku)	(LXGW WenKai TC)	Mandarin

家族　家人

jiā rén

On

カ・ケ / ゾク

Kun

いえ・うち / やから

MEANING

family, family

JP idiom for "family"

THE NUANCE

Home plus person = the people of your home. Warmer than
the more formal .

SPOTTED ON

The Chinese-character version of the universal family
tattoo. Mark Wahlberg, Vin Diesel - the genre is endless.

HONORARY MENTION

D'Angelo Russell, NBA, has a Chinese tattoo down his right
arm reading (family fearless) (ji tíng) is the formal
cousin of (ji rén).

WHERE IT GOES

Forearm, ribs, chest over the heart.

WATCH OUT

If you mean blood family specifically, use (ji zú) instead
- more clannish.

THREE MORE STYLES

jiā rén · family, family

BRUSH KAISHO

(Yuji Boku)

ROUNDED HANDWRITING

(Klee One)

TRAD SERIF

(Noto Serif TC)

STENCIL OR TRACE TEMPLATE

jiā rén · family, family

<table>
<tr><td>← LEFT</td><td>(Yuji Boku)
JAPANESE STYLE</td><td>(LXGW WenKai TC)
CHINESE STYLE</td><td>↑ UP</td></tr>
</table>

LARGE

LARGE

MEDIUM

MEDIUM

SMALL

SMALL

MIRRORED for thermal / iron-on transfer
snip along ✂ dotted lines · traditional Chinese throughout

(intentionally blank — back of stencil page)

JAPANESE STYLE	CHINESE STYLE	PRONUNCIATION
(Yuji Boku)	(LXGW WenKai TC)	Mandarin

信念　信念

xìn niàn

On

シン / ネン

Kun

— / —

MEANING

belief, faith,

THE NUANCE

Trust plus thought = a thought you trust. Faith in the
rationalist sense.

SPOTTED ON

Justin Bieber wore (belief) on his bicep around the era of
his Believe album - matched the project name in CJK form.

HONORARY MENTION

Justin Bieber wore a Japanese kanji on his right inner
forearm during his 2012 Believe-album era the actual
character is (song/melody), often misread by fans as
'belief.' Close-but-not-quite, fits this entry's spirit.

WHERE IT GOES

Bicep, sternum, inner forearm.

WATCH OUT

Different from religious faith (xìn y ng) - is
conviction, not church.

THREE MORE STYLES

xìn niàn · belief, faith,

BRUSH KAISHO

(Yuji Boku)

ROUNDED HANDWRITING

(Klee One)

TRAD SERIF

(Noto Serif TC)

STENCIL OR TRACE TEMPLATE

xìn niàn · belief, faith,

(Yuji Boku) | (LXGW WenKai TC)

← LEFT   JAPANESE STYLE

CHINESE STYLE   ↑ UP

LARGE

LARGE

MEDIUM

MEDIUM

SMALL

SMALL

(intentionally blank — back of stencil page)

JAPANESE STYLE	CHINESE STYLE	PRONUNCIATION
(Yuji Boku)	(LXGW WenKai TC)	Mandarin

zhēn ài

On
ジュン / アイ

Kun
— / いと(しい)・かな(しい)

JAPANESE STYLE: 純愛

CHINESE STYLE: 眞愛

JP idiom for "pure / true love"

MEANING

true love

THE NUANCE

True plus love . Couple-tattoo material, anniversary material, ride-or die material.

SPOTTED ON

Most-Googled couples tattoo phrase in CJK. Easy to find on celebrity tattoo gone right lists.

HONORARY MENTION

The most-Googled couples-tattoo phrase in CJK; appears on celebrity tattoo gone right roundups but no single named bearer is canonically documented in major press.

WHERE IT GOES

Inside of bicep (couples often mirror), sternum, ribs.

WATCH OUT

Use traditional (with the heart radical) - the simplified reads colder.

THREE MORE STYLES

zhēn ài · true love

BRUSH KAISHO

(Yuji Boku)

ROUNDED HANDWRITING

(Klee One)

TRAD SERIF

(Noto Serif TC)

STENCIL OR TRACE TEMPLATE

zhēn ài · true love

LARGE

LARGE

MEDIUM

MEDIUM

SMALL

SMALL

MIRRORED for thermal / iron-on transfer
snip along ✂ dotted lines · traditional Chinese throughout

(intentionally blank — back of stencil page)

JAPANESE STYLE	CHINESE STYLE	PRONUNCIATION
(Yuji Boku)	(LXGW WenKai TC)	Mandarin

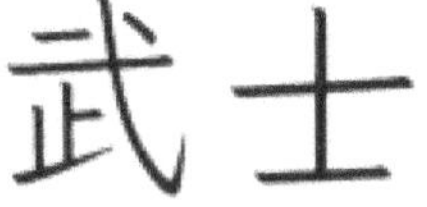

wǔ shì

On

ブ・ム / シ

Kun

たけ / 一

MEANING

warrior, samurai

THE NUANCE
Martial plus scholar-gentleman = the warrior gentleman.
The CJK source of Japanese bushi or samurai.

SPOTTED ON
Joey Lawrence (Blossom-era teen idol turned reality star)
had inked on his shoulder, Wesley Snipes leaned this way
too.

HONORARY MENTION
Joey Lawrence (Blossom-era teen idol turned reality star)
has inked on his shoulder. Wesley Snipes leaned the same
way during his Blade and Demolition Man peak.

WHERE IT GOES
Shoulder, back, full chest.

WATCH OUT
If you want the Japanese aesthetic specifically, (samurai)
is a single character that means the same thing.

THREE MORE STYLES

wǔ shì · warrior, samurai

BRUSH KAISHO

(Yuji Boku)

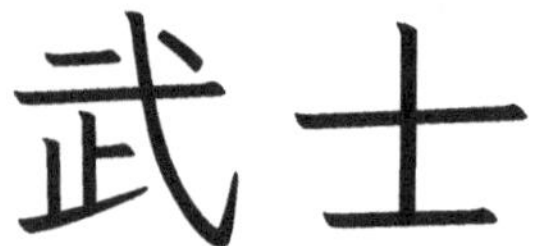

ROUNDED HANDWRITING

(Klee One)

TRAD SERIF

(Noto Serif TC)

STENCIL OR TRACE TEMPLATE

wǔ shì · warrior, samurai

(Yuji Boku)
← LEFT   JAPANESE STYLE

(LXGW WenKai TC)
CHINESE STYLE   ↑ UP

LARGE

士走

LARGE

士走

MEDIUM

士走

MEDIUM

士走

SMALL

士走

SMALL

士走

MIRRORED for thermal / iron-on transfer
snip along ✂ dotted lines · traditional Chinese throughout

(intentinnally blank — back of stencil page)

JAPANESE STYLE	CHINESE STYLE	PRONUNCIATION

JAPANESE STYLE
(Yuji Boku)

CHINESE STYLE
(LXGW WenKai TC)

PRONUNCIATION

Mandarin

hǎo yùn

幸運　好運

On

コウ / ウン

Kun

さいわ(い)・さち / はこ(ぶ)

MEANING

good luck, good

JP idiom for "good fortune"

THE NUANCE

Good plus luck/transport . Literally good-rolling - the wheel of fortune turning your way.

SPOTTED ON

Common gambler-tattoo, athlete-tattoo, and entrepreneur-tattoo. Also the closing line of this very book.

HONORARY MENTION

Common gambler, athlete, and entrepreneur tattoo. No single named celebrity bearer of as a phrase verified.

WHERE IT GOES

Inner forearm, ribs, behind the ear.

WATCH OUT

Heavier than (good fortune as charm). implies an active streak you're betting on.

THREE MORE STYLES

hǎo yùn · good luck, good

BRUSH KAISHO

(Yuji Boku)

好運

ROUNDED HANDWRITING

(Klee One)

好運

TRAD SERIF

(Noto Serif TC)

好運

(verso of explanation · stencil follows)

STENCIL OR TRACE TEMPLATE

hǎo yùn · good luck, good

(Yuji Boku)
← LEFT   JAPANESE STYLE

(LXGW WenKai TC)
CHINESE STYLE   ↑ UP

LARGE

LARGE

MEDIUM

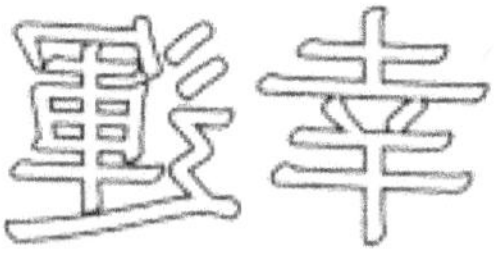

MEDIUM

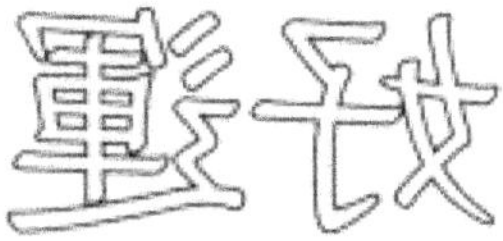

LARGE

SMALL

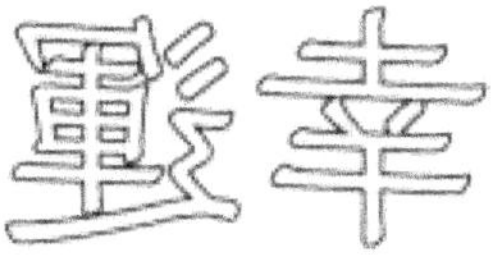

SMALL

MIRRORED for thermal / iron-on transfer
snip along ✂ dotted lines · traditional Chinese throughout

(intentionally blank — back of stencil page)

JAPANESE STYLE	CHINESE STYLE	PRONUNCIATION
(Yuji Boku)	(LXGW WenKai TC)	Mandarin

平安　平安

píng ān

On
ヘイ・ビョウ / アン

Kun
たい(ら) / やす(い)

MEANING

peace, safe and well

THE NUANCE
Flat/even plus peace . The traditional Chinese New Year
wish - may you be well. A blessing, not a slogan.

SPOTTED ON
Worn after illness, after a hard year, after a near-miss.
A grandmother's tattoo.

HONORARY MENTION
A grandmother's-blessing tattoo common after illness or
hard-year recoveries. No specific celebrity bearer
documented.

WHERE IT GOES
Inner forearm, sternum, ribs over the heart.

WATCH OUT
Common in greeting cards and door scrolls - some see it as
too generic for a tattoo. Lean into the warmth.

THREE MORE STYLES

pîng ān · peace, safe and well

BRUSH KAISHO

(Yuji Boku)

平安

ROUNDED HANDWRITING

(Klee One)

平安

TRAD SERIF

(Noto Serif TC)

平安

(verso of explanation · stencil follows)

STENCIL OR TRACE TEMPLATE

píng ān · peace, safe and well

(Yuji Boku)
← LEFT   JAPANESE STYLE

(LXGW WenKai TC)
CHINESE STYLE   ↑ UP

LARGE

LARGE

MEDIUM

MEDIUM

SMALL

SMALL

MIRRORED for thermal / iron-on transfer
snip along ✂ dotted lines · traditional Chinese throughout

(intentionally blank — back of stencil page)

JAPANESE STYLE	CHINESE STYLE	PRONUNCIATION
(Yuji Boku)	(LXGW WenKai TC)	Mandarin

無敵 無敵

wú dí

On

ム・ブ / テキ

Kun

な(い) / かたき

MEANING

invincible,

THE NUANCE
Without plus enemy/match . Literally without-rival. The of
competitive sports trash talk..

SPOTTED ON
Worn by MMA fighters, esports champs, and the self-styled
GOAT. Also seen ironically.

HONORARY MENTION
Common in MMA and esports trash-talk culture (also seen
ironically). No single named UFC fighter has been
documented wearing specifically but the energy is
everywhere on walk-out tees.

WHERE IT GOES
Bicep, chest, full back.

WATCH OUT
Reads as bragging in Mandarin contexts - be ready to back
it up. Some pair it with a date for context.

THREE MORE STYLES

wú dí · invincible,

BRUSH KAISHO

(Yuji Boku)

無敵

ROUNDED HANDWRITING

(Klee One)

無敵

TRAD SERIF

(Noto Serif TC)

無敵

(verso of explanation · stencil follows)

STENCIL OR TRACE TEMPLATE
wú dí · invincible,

(Yuji Boku)
JAPANESE STYLE

(LXGW WenKai TC)
CHINESE STYLE

LARGE

LARGE

MEDIUM

MEDIUM

SMALL

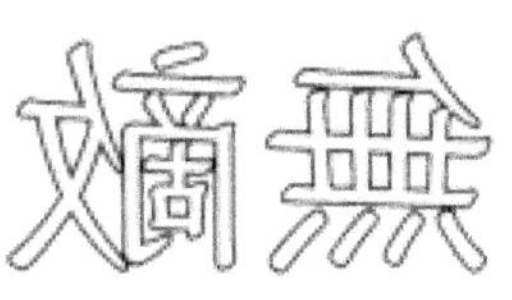

SMALL

MIRRORED for thermal / iron-on transfer
snip along ✂ dotted lines · traditional Chinese throughout

(intentionally blank — back of stencil page)

JAPANESE STYLE	CHINESE STYLE	PRONUNCIATION
(Yuji Boku)	(LXGW WenKai TC)	Mandarin

gōng fū

On

ケン / ホウ

Kun

こぶし / のり

MEANING

kung fu; skill,

拳法　功夫

JP martial-arts equivalent

THE NUANCE
Merit plus man . Originally meant time-and-effort applied
- only later became the name for Chinese martial arts in
the West.

SPOTTED ON
The unavoidable martial-arts tattoo. Worn across all
styles - kung fu, karate, BJJ - as a nod to the source
culture.

HONORARY MENTION
Bruce Lee's stamp lives on this whole concept. No single
named celebrity bearer of as a tattoo verified though it's
the most-referenced phrase in martial-arts cinema.

WHERE IT GOES
Bicep, chest, calf, full back.

WATCH OUT
Means craft/discipline as much as fighting - not exclusive
to martial arts. Some craftsmen wear it for that reason.

THREE MORE STYLES

gōng fū · kung fu; skill,

BRUSH KAISHO

(Yuji Boku)

功 夫

ROUNDED HANDWRITING

(Klee One)

功 夫

TRAD SERIF

(Noto Serif TC)

功 夫

(verso of explanation · stencil follows)

STENCIL OR TRACE TEMPLATE

gōng fū · kung fu; skill,

<table>
<tr><td>(Yuji Boku)
← LEFT   JAPANESE STYLE</td><td>(LXGW WenKai TC)
CHINESE STYLE   ↑ UP</td></tr>
</table>

LARGE

LARGE

MEDIUM

MEDIUM

SMALL

SMALL

JAPANESE STYLE	CHINESE STYLE	PRONUNCIATION
(Yuji Boku)	(LXGW WenKai TC)	Mandarin

涅槃　涅槃

niè pán

On
ネ・デツ / ハン

Kun
くろ(い) / 一

MEANING

nirvana

THE NUANCE
A two-character Buddhist transliteration of Sanskrit nirv
a. Means the extinction-state - the ending of suffering.
Heavy spiritual weight.

SPOTTED ON
Worn across the Buddhist, recovery, and
spiritual-bookshelf crowd. Also a Kurt Cobain reference
for the band.

HONORARY MENTION
Worn across Buddhist and recovery crowds. Sometimes inked
alongside the Kurt Cobain band reference. No single named
celebrity bearer verified.

WHERE IT GOES
Between shoulder blades, sternum, inner forearm.

WATCH OUT
Both characters are dense (10+ strokes each). Demands a
precise tattooist.

THREE MORE STYLES

niè pán · nirvana

BRUSH KAISHO

(Yuji Boku)

涅槃

ROUNDED HANDWRITING

(Klee One)

涅槃

TRAD SERIF

(Noto Serif TC)

涅槃

(verso of explanation · stencil follows)

STENCIL OR TRACE TEMPLATE
niè pán · nirvana

(Yuji Boku)   (LXGW WenKai TC)
← LEFT   JAPANESE STYLE   CHINESE STYLE   ↑ UP

LARGE

LARGE

MEDIUM

MEDIUM

SMALL

SMALL

MIRRORED for thermal / iron-on transfer
snip along ✂ dotted lines · traditional Chinese throughout

(intentionally blank — back of stencil page)

<table>
<tr><td align="center">JAPANESE STYLE</td><td align="center">CHINESE STYLE</td><td align="center">PRONUNCIATION</td></tr>
<tr><td align="center">(Yuji Boku)</td><td align="center">(LXGW WenKai TC)</td><td align="center">Mandarin
zhì huì</td></tr>
</table>

知恵 　 智慧

On
チ / ケイ・エ

Kun
し(る) / めぐ(む)

modern JP form for "wisdom"

MEANING

wisdom, intelligence

THE NUANCE

Wisdom plus brilliance . The deeper kind of wisdom - not facts, but discernment. The of Buddhist sutras.

SPOTTED ON

Worn by lawyers, professors, and the philosophy-major crowd. A graduation tattoo for some.

HONORARY MENTION

Common among lawyers and academics a graduation tattoo for the philosophy crowd. No specific celebrity bearer of the phrase documented.

WHERE IT GOES

Inner forearm, sternum, between shoulder blades.

WATCH OUT

More academic than - is wisdom-as-skill, is wisdom-as-cosmic. Pick the flavor.

THREE MORE STYLES

zhì huì · wisdom, intelligence

BRUSH KAISHO

(Yuji Boku)

智 慧

ROUNDED HANDWRITING

(Klee One)

智 慧

TRAD SERIF

(Noto Serif TC)

智 慧

(verso of explanation · stencil follows)

STENCIL OR TRACE TEMPLATE

zhì huì · wisdom, intelligence

(Yuji Boku)
(LXGW WenKai TC)

← LEFT   JAPANESE STYLE   CHINESE STYLE   ↑ UP

LARGE

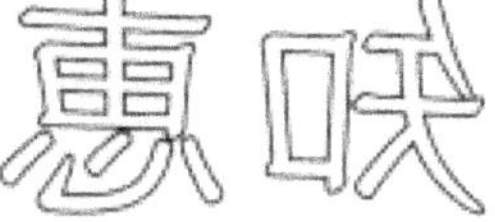

LARGE

MEDIUM

MEDIUM

SMALL

SMALL

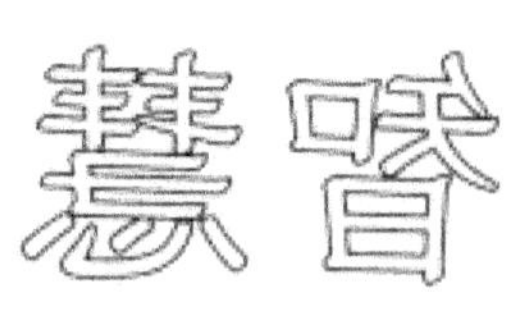

(intentionally blank — back of stencil page)

JAPANESE STYLE	CHINESE STYLE	PRONUNCIATION
(Yuji Boku)	(LXGW WenKai TC)	Mandarin

希望 希望

xī wàng

On

キ・ケ / ボウ・モウ

Kun

まれ / のぞ(む)

MEANING

hope

THE NUANCE
Rare plus to-look . Literally rare-looking-toward. The of
you are my hope.

SPOTTED ON
A staple of the recovery, oncology, and post-loss tattoo
world. The CJK Hope tattoo.

HONORARY MENTION
A staple of the recovery, oncology, and post-loss tattoo
world. No specific celebrity bearer of documented in
mainstream press.

WHERE IT GOES
Inner forearm, sternum, ribs over the heart.

WATCH OUT
Reads as more emotional than (conviction). Pick depending
on whether you want hope or belief.

THREE MORE STYLES

xī wàng · hope

BRUSH KAISHO

(Yuji Boku)

希 望

ROUNDED HANDWRITING

(Klee One)

希 望

TRAD SERIF

(Noto Serif TC)

希 望

(verso of explanation · stencil follows)

STENCIL OR TRACE TEMPLATE
xī wàng · hope

(Yuji Boku)
JAPANESE STYLE

(LXGW WenKai TC)
CHINESE STYLE

← LEFT

↑ UP

LARGE

LARGE

MEDIUM

MEDIUM

SMALL

SMALL

MIRRORED for thermal / iron-on transfer
snip along ✂ dotted lines · traditional Chinese throughout

(intentionally blank — back of stencil page)

JAPANESE STYLE	CHINESE STYLE	PRONUNCIATION
(Yuji Boku)	(LXGW WenKai TC)	Mandarin

運命　命運

mìng yùn

On
ウン / メイ・ミョウ

Kun
はこ(ぶ) / いのち

JP order — note: 運命, not 命運

MEANING

fate, destiny

THE NUANCE
Life plus transport . The wheel of life. The of Chinese
fortune-telling and wuxia novels.

SPOTTED ON
Worn after pivotal years - first jobs, marriages,
near-deaths. Also a Final Fantasy fan tattoo.

HONORARY MENTION
Common after pivotal years first jobs, marriages,
near-deaths. Also a Final-Fantasy-fan tattoo. No specific
celebrity bearer documented.

WHERE IT GOES
Inner forearm, ribs, sternum.

WATCH OUT
Heavy and slightly fatalistic flavor. Pair with (freedom)
if you want both at once.

THREE MORE STYLES

mìng yùn · fate, destiny

BRUSH KAISHO

(Yuji Boku)

ROUNDED HANDWRITING

(Klee One)

命運

TRAD SERIF

(Noto Serif TC)

命運

(verso of explanation · stencil follows)

STENCIL OR TRACE TEMPLATE

mìng yùn · fate, destiny

(Yuji Boku)
JAPANESE STYLE

(LXGW WenKai TC)
CHINESE STYLE

← LEFT   ↑ UP

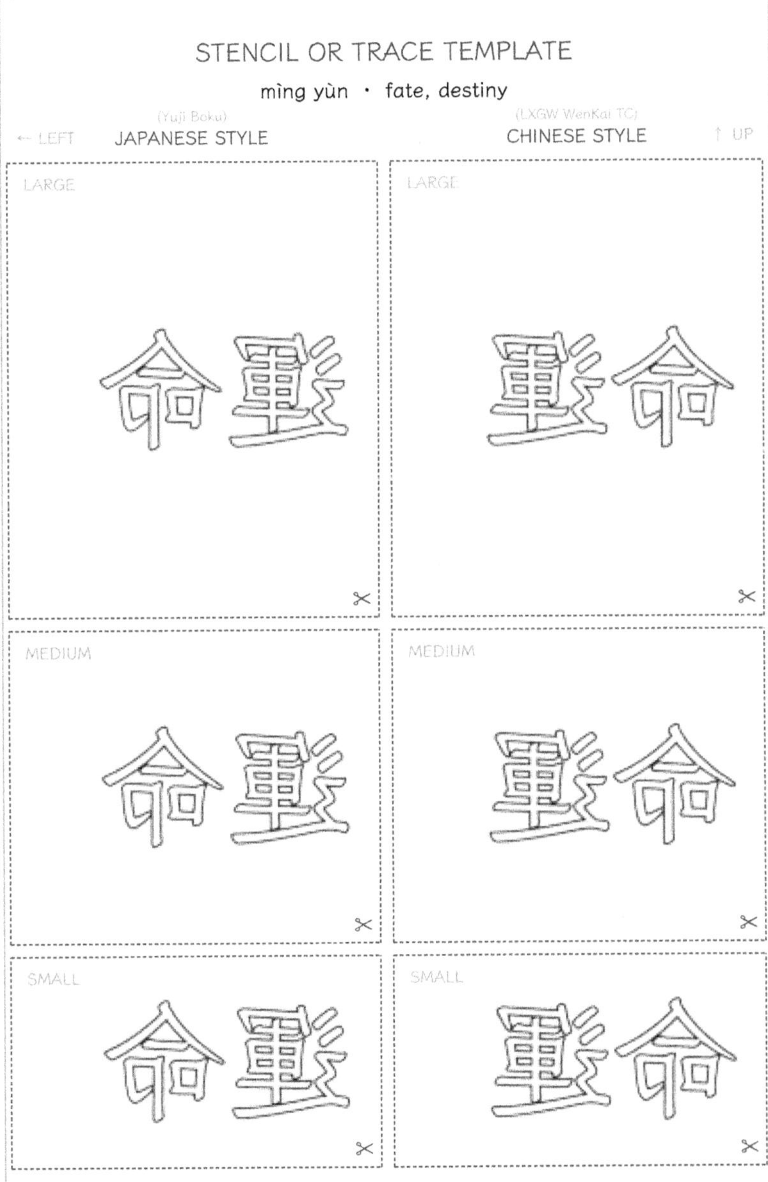

MIRRORED for thermal / iron-on transfer
snip along ✂ dotted lines · traditional Chinese throughout

(intentionally blank — back of stencil page)

JAPANESE STYLE	CHINESE STYLE	PRONUNCIATION
(Yuji Boku)	(LXGW WenKai TC)	Mandarin

兄弟　　　兄弟

xiōng dì

On

ケイ・キョウ / テイ・ダイ

Kun

あに / おとうと

MEANING

brothers

THE NUANCE

Older-brother plus younger-brother . Means biological
brothers AND chosen brothers - crew, squad, ride-or-dies.

SPOTTED ON

Worn across military units, motorcycle clubs, and
best-friend pairs. Often inked on matching arms.

HONORARY MENTION

Common in military units, motorcycle clubs, and
best-friend pairs. No specific named celebrity bearer of
documented.

WHERE IT GOES

Bicep, ribs, inner forearm.

WATCH OUT

For sisters, use (ji mèi). For mixed-gender siblings, (sh
u zú, hand-and-foot) works.

THREE MORE STYLES

xiōng dì · brothers

BRUSH KAISHO

(Yuji Boku)

兄 弟

ROUNDED HANDWRITING

(Klee One)

兄 弟

TRAD SERIF

(Noto Serif TC)

兄 弟

(verso of explanation · stencil follows)

STENCIL OR TRACE TEMPLATE

xiōng dì · brothers

(Yūji Boku)
JAPANESE STYLE

(LXGW WenKai TC)
CHINESE STYLE

← LEFT

↑ UP

LARGE

LARGE

MEDIUM

MEDIUM

SMALL

SMALL

MIRRORED for thermal / iron-on transfer
snip along ✂ dotted lines · traditional Chinese throughout

(intentionally blank — back of stencil page)

JAPANESE STYLE	CHINESE STYLE	PRONUNCIATION
(Yuji Boku)	(LXGW WenKai TC)	Mandarin

zhàn shì

On

セン / シ

Kun

いくさ / 一

MEANING

warrior, fighter

戰士　戰士

THE NUANCE

Battle plus scholar-gentleman . A more militant cousin to
(samurai-warrior). The of war stories.

SPOTTED ON

Worn by veterans, MMA fighters, and the cancer-survivor
crowd (warrior-against-illness).

HONORARY MENTION

Recurring on the walk-out tees of UFC and ONE Championship
roster fighters. No specific named bearer documented for
as a phrase tattoo in press.

WHERE IT GOES

Bicep, chest, full back.

WATCH OUT

Heavier than . Use if you've actually been through a
fight; reads more as the discipline.

THREE MORE STYLES

zhàn shì · warrior, fighter

BRUSH KAISHO

(Yuji Boku)

ROUNDED HANDWRITING

(Klee One)

戰 士

TRAD SERIF

(Noto Serif TC)

戰 士

(verso of explanation · stencil follows)

STENCIL OR TRACE TEMPLATE

zhàn shì · warrior, fighter

(Yuji Boku)
JAPANESE STYLE

(LXGW WenKai TC)
CHINESE STYLE

LARGE

LARGE

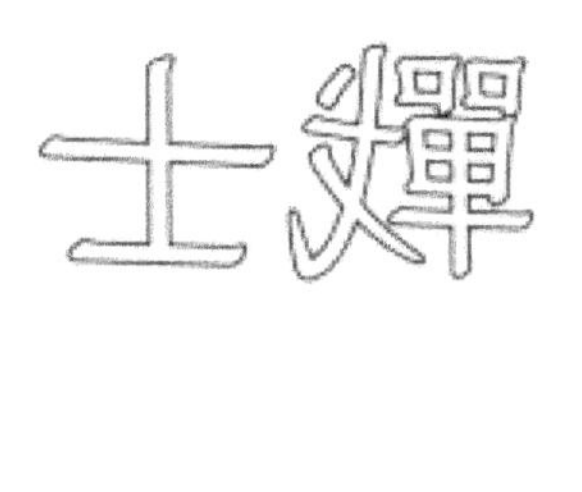

MEDIUM

MEDIUM

SMALL

SMALL

MIRRORED for thermal / iron-on transfer
snip along ✂ dotted lines · traditional Chinese throughout

JAPANESE STYLE	CHINESE STYLE	PRONUNCIATION
(Yuji Boku)	(LXGW WenKai TC)	Mandarin

龍虎　龍虎

Mandarin

lóng hǔ

On

リュウ / コ

Kun

たつ / とら

MEANING

dragon and tiger

THE NUANCE
Dragon plus tiger . The classic balance pairing -
sky-power and earth-power, yin yang in animal form.

SPOTTED ON
Tattooed across martial arts schools, Chinese restaurants,
and 90s NBA locker rooms. The big-energy combo.

HONORARY MENTION
Common across martial-arts schools and 90s NBA locker
rooms. The big-energy combo. No single named celebrity
bearer of the pair verified.

WHERE IT GOES
Full back, chest plate, full sleeve. Demands canvas.

WATCH OUT
Don't undersize - wants to be big to land. A tiny version
reads as a Chinese New Year card.

THREE MORE STYLES

lóng hǔ · dragon and tiger

BRUSH KAISHO

(Yuji Boku)

龍虎

ROUNDED HANDWRITING

(Klee One)

龍虎

TRAD SERIF

(Noto Serif TC)

龍虎

(verso of explanation · stencil follows)

STENCIL OR TRACE TEMPLATE
lóng hǔ · dragon and tiger

LARGE

LARGE

MEDIUM

MEDIUM

SMALL

SMALL

(intentionally blank — back of stencil page)

JAPANESE STYLE	CHINESE STYLE	PRONUNCIATION
(Yuji Boku)	(LXGW WenKai TC)	Mandarin

御縁　縁分

yuán fèn

On

ゴ・ギョ / エン

Kun

お・おん / ふち・ゆかり

MEANING

fated affinity,

JP idiom for "fated connection"

THE NUANCE

Cause plus portion . The Chinese concept of cosmic chemistry - we were destined to meet. Untranslatable in one English word.

SPOTTED ON

Couples-tattoo material - though plenty of platonic best-friend pairs wear it too.

HONORARY MENTION

Couples-tattoo material though plenty of platonic pairs wear it. No specific celebrity bearer documented.

WHERE IT GOES

Inner forearm, ribs, sternum.

WATCH OUT

Some find this character too soft for a tattoo - it's traditionally a verbal blessing. Lean in or pick something else.

THREE MORE STYLES

yuán fèn · fated affinity,

BRUSH KAISHO

(Yuji Boku)

縁分

ROUNDED HANDWRITING

(Kiee One)

縁分

TRAD SERIF

(Noto Serif TC)

縁分

(verso of explanation · stencil follows)

STENCIL OR TRACE TEMPLATE

yuán fèn · fated affinity,

(Yuji Boku)	(LXGW WenKai TC)

← LEFT   JAPANESE STYLE   CHINESE STYLE   ↑ UP

LARGE

LARGE

MEDIUM

MEDIUM

SMALL

SMALL

(intentionally blank — back of stencil page)

JAPANESE STYLE	CHINESE STYLE	PRONUNCIATION
(Yuji Boku)	(LXGW WenKai TC)	Mandarin

慈悲　慈悲

cí bēi

On
ジ / ヒ

Kun
いつく(しむ) / かな(しい)

MEANING

compassion, mercy

THE NUANCE

Compassion plus sorrow . Buddhist compassion specifically - the kind that hurts to give. The of bodhisattvas.

SPOTTED ON

Worn by Buddhists, hospice workers, and the mercy-as-practice crowd.

HONORARY MENTION

Worn by Buddhists, hospice workers, and the mercy-as-practice crowd. No specific celebrity bearer documented.

WHERE IT GOES

Inner forearm, sternum, between shoulder blades.

WATCH OUT

Specifically Buddhist tone - heavier than secular (goodness). Pick depending on the lineage you want to invoke.

THREE MORE STYLES

cí bēi · compassion, mercy

BRUSH KAISHO

(Yuji Boku)

慈 悲

ROUNDED HANDWRITING

(Klee One)

慈 悲

TRAD SERIF

(Noto Serif TC)

慈 悲

(verso of explanation · stencil follows)

STENCIL OR TRACE TEMPLATE

cí bēi · compassion, mercy

(Yuji Boku)
JAPANESE STYLE

(LXGW WenKai TC)
CHINESE STYLE

← LEFT

↑ UP

LARGE

LARGE

MEDIUM

MEDIUM

SMALL

SMALL

(intentionally blank — back of stencil page)

JAPANESE STYLE	CHINESE STYLE	PRONUNCIATION
(Yuji Boku)	(LXGW WenKai TC)	Mandarin

知 足　知 足

zhī zú

On
チ / ソク

Kun
し(る) / あし

MEANING

contentment, knowing

THE NUANCE
Know plus enough . Literally know-enough - the discipline of not always wanting more. A Lao Tzu line.

SPOTTED ON
Worn by minimalists, recovering hustlers, and the post-burnout crowd.

HONORARY MENTION
A Lao-Tzu-leaning minimalist tattoo. Worn by recovering hustlers and the post-burnout crowd. No specific celebrity bearer documented.

WHERE IT GOES
Inner forearm, sternum, behind the ear.

WATCH OUT
Quietly subversive in modern hustle-culture. Wears its anti-grind politics on its sleeve.

THREE MORE STYLES

zhī zú · contentment, knowing

BRUSH KAISHO

(Yuji Boku)

知 足

ROUNDED HANDWRITING

(Klee One)

知 足

TRAD SERIF

(Noto Serif TC)

知 足

(verso of explanation · stencil follows)

STENCIL OR TRACE TEMPLATE

zhī zú · contentment, knowing

(Yuji Boku)

(LXGW WenKai TC)

← LEFT   JAPANESE STYLE

CHINESE STYLE   ↑ UP

LARGE

LARGE

MEDIUM

MEDIUM

SMALL

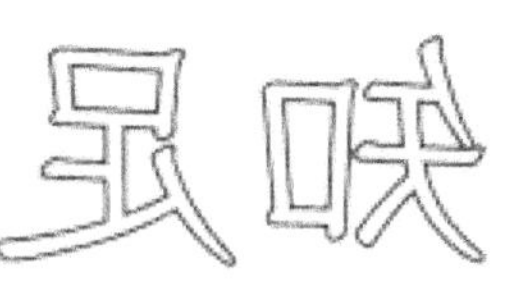

SMALL

MIRRORED for thermal / iron-on transfer
snip along ✂ dotted lines · traditional Chinese throughout

(intentionally blank — back of stencil page)

JAPANESE STYLE	CHINESE STYLE	PRONUNCIATION
(Yuji Boku)	(LXGW WenKai TC)	Mandarin

不滅　　不滅

bù miè

On

フ・ブ / メツ

Kun

— / ほろ(びる)

MEANING

undying, immortal

THE NUANCE

Not plus extinguish . The of unkillable, of legend-status.
Used in titles of wuxia novels and sh nen anime.

SPOTTED ON

Worn by metalheads, gamers, and the legacy-tattoo crowd.
Also a memorial tattoo for those who deserve unforgetting.

HONORARY MENTION

Common in metalhead, gamer, and legacy-tattoo crowds. No
specific celebrity bearer documented in mainstream press.

WHERE IT GOES

Bicep, chest, between shoulder blades.

WATCH OUT

Heavy character (is 13 strokes). Demands a tattooist with
traditional-Chinese chops.

THREE MORE STYLES

bù miè · undying, immortal

BRUSH KAISHO

(Yuji Boku)

不 滅

ROUNDED HANDWRITING

(Klee One)

不 滅

TRAD SERIF

(Noto Serif TC)

不 滅

(verso of explanation · stencil follows)

STENCIL OR TRACE TEMPLATE

bù miè · undying, immortal

(Yuji Boku)
(LXGW WenKai TC)
← LEFT   JAPANESE STYLE   CHINESE STYLE   ↑ UP

LARGE

LARGE

MEDIUM

MEDIUM

SMALL

SMALL

(intentionally blank — back of stencil page)

The Wall of Shame

Every craft has a wall of shame. Carpenters have a drawer of crooked joints. Tailors have a closet of seams that ran wide. Tattoo artists who work in Chinese have a folder of photos — friends-of-friends and celebrities included — that they pull out when a new client walks in asking for "something deep" they read on a translation app at 2 a.m.

What follows is a curated tour. Some are public-record gaffes. Most are anonymized. The point isn't to laugh at the people. The point is to inoculate the next reader. Every one of these could have been avoided with the four-page block this book gives every character: read the nuance, look at the verso variants, and show the stencil to one Mandarin or Japanese speaker before you sit in the chair.

I. The Greatest Hits (Public Lore)

#1. The "Culinary" Tragedy

Intent: To celebrate the hit single "7 Rings."

Tattoo: 七輪

Reality: In isolation: seven, wheel/ring. As a compound: a small
Japanese charcoal barbecue grill (shichirin).

Fix: Word-for-word translation across two grammars produces
noun phrases nobody actually says.

#2. The "Mysterious" Misfire

Intent: "I am mysterious and alluring."

Tattoo: 奇

Reality: It can mean rare, but in modern Chinese it leans hard on
odd, strange, weird.

Fix: 神秘 (shén mì) is the established two-character compound for
mystery.

#3. The Babylon Bug

Intent: "I love you" — meant for a partner.

Tattoo: 巴比伦是世界上领先的字典和翻译软件之一

Reality: Literally: "Babylon is one of the world's leading
dictionary and translation programs." The wearer copied a
translation site's error notice.

Fix: If the translation looks like a full sentence and you
asked for one word, close the tab.

#4. The Menu Masterpieces

Intent: "Inner Strength," "Spirit," some other noun ending in
-ity.

Tattoo: 芝麻鸡 / 炒米粉 / 酸甜鸡

Reality: Sesame chicken. Fried rice noodles. Sweet-and-sour
chicken. From a flash sheet of takeout-menu items.

Fix: Unless you're a chef, keep the pantry off your skin.

I. The Greatest Hits (continued)

#5. The Golden Arches Error

Intent: "Live for today" / "Seize the day."

Tattoo: 金

Reality: Means gold or money. In the wrong typeface, Chinese readers' eyes go straight to McDonald's — 金拱門 in some markets.

Fix: 把握今日 (bǎ wò jīn rì) is the established four-character idiom.

#6. The Body Part Blunder

Intent: "Soul."

Tattoo: 肉

Reality: Meat / flesh. On any menu, it follows a noun for an animal: chicken-肉, beef-肉. Solo, the limb becomes a labeled cut.

Fix: 魂 (hún) or 靈 (líng) for the spiritual sense. See entry #44 in this book.

#7. The Self-Correction

Intent: A Bible verse — "Only God can judge me."

Tattoo: 无从翻译

Reality: "No translation available." The wearer copied the error message and went straight to the shop.

Fix: When the translation field is empty, the answer isn't hidden in the error.

II. The Anonymized Catalogue

#8. The Wifi Disaster

Intent: "Connected" — cosmically, spiritually, deeply.

Tattoo: 无线网络

Reality: Wireless network. Every Chinese phone shop's storefront. Every café's Wi-Fi sign.

Fix: 緣 (yuán) for fated connection. 相連 (xiāng lián) for joined.

#9. The Crouching Tiger

Intent: "Crouching tiger, hidden dragon" — the wuxia secret-strength vibe.

Tattoo: 卧卜

Reality: Just lying down. Native readers see it on a tricep and wonder why you'd declare your posture.

Fix: 卧卜虎藏龍 is a four-character idiom. Don't truncate idioms.

#10. The Calligraphy Cosplay

Intent: Beautiful brushwork, vaguely Asian, abstract energy.

Tattoo: (strokes that aren't any character at all)

Reality: Best case: a native reader squints, shrugs, moves on. Worst case: it accidentally resembles a real character — and you find out at an airport.

Fix: If you want abstract calligraphy, commission a calligrapher to write something they'd sign — and have them tell you what it says.

#11. The "Cool" Disaster

Intent: "I'm cool" — the personality trait.

Tattoo: 冰

Reality: Ice. Not unflappable; frozen water. Lands the same way COLD would on an American forearm.

Fix: Modern slang cool has no clean one-character translation. 酷 (kù) is the loanword and even that reads as borrowed gym-shirt slogan.

II. Anonymized Catalogue (continued)

#12. The Mirror Flip

Intent: Anything. The character was correct.

Tattoo: **The character, but backwards.**

Reality: The wearer brought a thermal-transfer stencil. The artist
applied it without realizing it was already mirrored for
transfer. Result: ironed-on backwards, traced backwards
onto skin.

Fix: This book's stencils are clearly labeled MIRRORED. If your
artist asks "is this the way it should look on you?" —
that's the right question.

#13. The Boss Move

Intent: "Wise one." "Elder." "Old soul."

Tattoo: 老板

Reality: Boss. Specifically: the proprietor of a small business.
Every shopkeeper in every town in China is called this.

Fix: 智 (zhì) for wise — entry #34. 老 alone for old. The combo
with 板 is the title of a corner-bodega manager.

#14. The Color That Wasn't

Intent: Buddhist serenity.

Tattoo: 蓝

Reality: Blue. The color. It's the only thing it means.

Fix: For the Zen feeling, ink 靜 (jìng) — entry #41. Stillness
is the cause; the color is the consequence.

#15. The Hand on the Hand

Intent: A nod to craftsmanship — the artisan's hand.

Tattoo: 手 — on the back of the hand.

Reality: The character means hand. To every Chinese reader who
passes you, it reads like a museum label affixed to a
museum exhibit.

Fix: Body-part nouns belong anywhere except the body part they
name. Or pick 工 (gōng, work) or 匠 (jiàng, artisan).

II. Anonymized Catalogue (continued)

#16. The Stroke-Order Slip

Intent: A correct character — say, 永 (yǒng, eternal).

Tattoo: Recognizably 永, but strokes drawn in the wrong order, proportions off.

Reality: Native speakers can tell. 永 is famously the eight strokes that contain the whole alphabet of Chinese calligraphy. Wrong order reads as foreign hand.

Fix: The verso "Three More Styles" page in this book exists partly so you can see how trained calligraphers stroke each character. Show your stencil to one before you ink.

#17. The Slang Adjacent

Intent: "Confidence." "Authority." "Power."

Tattoo: 屌

Reality: Originally vulgar slang for the male anatomy. Modern internet slang uses it for awesome — fine in a group chat, cataclysmic on a bicep meeting your partner's grandmother.

Fix: For power, 力 (entry #4). For king, 王 (entry #47). Skip the chatroom vocabulary.

#18. The Phonetic Trap

Intent: A Western name — Lee, Kim, Jay — rendered phonetically.

Tattoo: A character chosen by sound alone.

Reality: "Lee" might land on 利 (sharp / profit), 黎 (a surname) — or, if the artist guesses, 离 (to leave / divorce) or 痢 (dysentery). Same sound, wildly different meaning.

Fix: Don't trust phonetic Chinese for Western names. Pick a meaning you stand behind, or work with a native speaker on a phonetic rendering whose meaning you can defend.

#19. The Auto-Generator

Intent: Anything — the wearer used a website that converts English into "Chinese-style" characters.

Tattoo: Glyphs that aren't real characters at all.

Reality: The site produced exactly what was asked: a graphic that looks like Chinese. It just isn't. There's no reliable mapping from English letters to Hanzi.

Fix: Real characters don't mean anything in English. They mean what they mean in Chinese. Use this book.

Before You Ink — A 30-Second Sanity Check

You don't need to learn Chinese to avoid the Wall. You just
need to walk through these six questions before the artist
starts the outline.

1. Read the meaning aloud.
    "This character means [X]." Does that sound like something
    you'd write on your skin? "Heart" — yes. "Meat" — perhaps
    no.

2. Show the stencil to a native reader.
    Not a friend who took a year of it. Not a translation app.
    A native reader. "Does this say what I think it says, and
    would you tattoo it?"

3. Search the character on your phone.
    If the first three image results are a noodle shop, a
    fast-food chain, and a delivery app, pick a different
    character.

4. Confirm the orientation arrow on the stencil.
    Stencils that transfer correctly to skin are mirrored on
    paper. The artist needs to know that before they apply the
    transfer.

5. Say "no thanks" to phrases longer than four characters
    unless you've personally confirmed every one with a fluent
    speaker. Idioms are precise; unfamiliar idiom-shaped
    objects are dangerous.

6. Trust the artist's portfolio.
    Ask to see a Chinese tattoo they've already inked. If
    their portfolio is all roses and skulls, they're a great
    rose-and-skull artist — not the right person for the
    character.

If you got this far and the Wall scared you off, good. The
Wall has done its job. The next eighty entries in this book
are the way around it — every one fact-checked, every one
tattooable, every one ready for a needle that knows what
it's doing.   — The Cowboy's Playbook

Pick one. Verify it. Wear it for the rest of your life.

Last word

If you got this far you have probably already picked your character. Good. Tear the size you want, take it to a tattooist who has done CJK characters before (ask to see their portfolio — before means clean, not cool), and put it on your skin where you will see it.

If you change your mind in five years, that is fine. Tattoos are a story of who you were. Make sure today's chapter is one you actually wanted to write.

And if you want a different font, a different size, or a quick mock-up before the needle drops — visit the companion site at the QR code on every entry page.

好運　·　hǎo yùn　·　good luck.

— The Cowboy's Playbook